Power Up Your Read-Alouds

Power Up Your Read-Alouds

Building Reading Excitement through Technology

Andrea Paganelli

LIBRARIES UNLIMITED®
An Imprint of ABC-CLIO, LLC
Santa Barbara, California • Denver, Colorado

Library of Congress Cataloging in Publication Control Number: 2019009850

ISBN: 978-1-4408-6520-6 (paperback)
      978-1-4408-6521-3 (ebook)

23 22 21 20 19   1 2 3 4 5

This book is also available as an eBook.
Libraries Unlimited
An Imprint of ABC-CLIO, LLC

ABC-CLIO, LLC
147 Castilian Drive
Santa Barbara, California 93117
www.abc-clio.com

This book is printed on acid-free paper ∞

Manufactured in the United States of America

*To my amazing family with appreciation for your support,
love, and chill time.*

Contents

Acknowledgments   xi

Introduction   xiii

Part One   Digital Read-Aloud: Creating the Experience   1

Chapter 1   Reading Aloud: A Brief History and the Issues and
                 Importance of Technology Inclusion   3
                 Reading Aloud: A Brief History   4
                 Reading Aloud Rocks the Ages!   5
                 Issues Related to Reading Aloud with Technology   7
                 The Importance of Technology Inclusion in Read-Aloud   12
                 Conclusion   13

Chapter 2   Knowing Your Audience Is Key to Planning
                 for Digital Read-Aloud   15
                 Using Technology-Infused Digital Read-Aloud
                     to Augment Engagement   17
                 Digital Read-Aloud Can Be Used to Promote
                     Lifelong Learning in Varied Ages and Demographics   18
                 Digital Read-Aloud Can Be Used One-on-One,
                     in Small Groups, or for Many   20
                 Digital Read-Aloud Can Be Cross-Curricular and
                     Embrace Any Subject   21
                 Conclusion   25

Chapter 3   Planning for a Digital Read-Aloud   27
                 Digital Resource Type Categories Available for
                     Digital Read-Aloud   27
                 Transmedia Resource Selection Process for Digital
                     Read-Aloud   31

Preparing to Present a Digital Read-Aloud　35
Planning for Cross-Curricular Digital Read-Aloud　37
Developing a Schedule for Cross-Curricular Digital
　Read-Aloud　38
Conclusion　39

Chapter 4　Implementation of the Digital Read-Aloud　41
Manage the Technology in Your Environment during
　the Digital Read-Aloud　41
Managing the Participants during the Digital
　Read-Aloud　45
Delivery of the Digital Read-Aloud　49
Conclusion　52

Chapter 5　Reflection on the Digital Read-Aloud　53
Examine the Digital Read-Aloud Experience and
　Methods of Improvement for Participants　54
Examine the Digital Read-Aloud Experience and
　Methods of Improvement of Delivery　54
Keep the Digital Read-Aloud Technology Experience
　Relevant through Continual Evaluation　55
Conclusion　59

Part Two　Examples of Digital Read-Aloud Experiences　61

Chapter 6　Language Arts　65
Pre-K　65
Elementary School　68
Middle School　70
High School　72
Lifelong Learner　75
Conclusion　78

Chapter 7　Math　79
Pre-K　80
Elementary School　82
Middle School　84
High School　86
Lifelong Learner　88
Conclusion　91

Chapter 8　Science　93
Pre-K　94
Elementary School　96
Middle School　98

	High School	100
	Lifelong Learner	102
	Conclusion	105
Chapter 9	History/Social Studies	107
	Pre-K	108
	Elementary School	110
	Middle School	112
	High School	114
	Lifelong Learner	116
	Conclusion	119
Chapter 10	Visual Performing Arts	121
	Pre-K	121
	Elementary School	124
	Middle School	126
	High School	128
	Lifelong Learner	130
	Conclusion	133
Conclusion		135
Glossary		137
Works Cited		141
Further Reading		145
Index		147

Acknowledgments

I would like to say thank you to . . .
    my family,
    everyone who has read to me,
    all educators and librarians,
    and specifically my colleagues and collaborators throughout the years.

Introduction

"I wish my learners would be as excited about reading as they are about technology" is a lament frequently sung by those who seek to support reading development. There is no debate that reading is fundamental and reading aloud strongly supports lifelong reading engagement. However, technology use is ubiquitous in our society, and engagement with technology is essential for our success. Reading and technology are in competition for our learners' attention. How can this tug-of-war be addressed? We can combine reading and technology through the use of read-aloud.

Through the combination of technology and read-aloud, facilitators can create engaging digital read-aloud programs to enhance the learning experience. Digital read-aloud can be used with multiple age groups, in a variety of settings, and with differing degrees of expense and technology complexity.

These options can be overwhelming. To meet this challenge, *Power Up Your Read-Alouds: Building Reading Excitement through Technology* is a research-based compendium of information on background, implementation, evaluation, and sustainability of the technology-infused read-aloud for reading support persons, school librarians, public librarians, instructional librarians, teachers, and professors that spans multiple ages and subjects and includes practical examples designed to engage.

This book has two distinct parts. Part 1 is Chapters 1–5 and includes: Reading Aloud: A Brief History and the Issues and Importance of Technology Inclusion, Knowing Your Audience Is Key to Planning for Digital Read-Aloud, Planning for a Digital Read-Aloud, Implementation of the Digital Read-Aloud, and Reflection on the Digital Read-Aloud. Part 2, Chapters 6–10, is devoted to read-aloud experience examples containing resource type category, group size, age level, and subject.

This book is for any reading support person, school librarian, public librarian, instructional librarian, teacher, and/or professor who wishes to foster reading as a lifelong pursuit for their learners.

Digital Read-Aloud: Creating the Experience

Reading Aloud: A Brief History and the Issues and Importance of Technology Inclusion

Reading aloud is a societal good.

Reading is a fundamental skill that will impact individuals throughout their lives. As a result, reading should begin early and persist throughout life to help ensure success (Anderson et al. 1985). Reading aloud is a shared experience that can cut across boundaries of age, race, gender, and economics to impact reading success. All come as they are to the read-aloud with equal opportunity to listen and learn. We have a shared and research-supported understanding that the read-aloud experience can positively impact myriad literacy development skills, motivation to read, and academic performance (Adams 1990; Anderson et al. 1985; Duursma, Augustyn, and Zuckerman 2008; Goldfield and Snow 1984; Keller 2012; Krashen 2004; Ross, McKechnie, and Rothbauer 2006; Trelease 2006).

A few of the early reading skills impacted are letter recognition, an understanding that print represents the spoken word, book mechanics (holding and turning pages), basic story structure, syntax, and grammar (Duursma, Augustyn, and Zuckerman 2008). Reading aloud can expose and connect learners to powerful concepts such as story elements, genres, vocabulary, authors, and illustrators. Reading aloud encourages vocabulary building. Beyond encouraging exposure to vocabulary-building text, as an added benefit, children's books contain 50 percent more rare words than popular television (Duursma, Augustyn, and Zuckerman 2008).

As a child of the predigital era, my read-aloud experience typically consisted of an advanced reader (like a parent or librarian), literature, and participants. I loved that engagement and would stare enthralled as the stories unfolded. The experience was a foundational, fond memory of youth. At its best, the read-aloud is a performance for participants designed to pique interest and drive engagement (Keller 2012; Paganelli 2016).

When an advanced reader models literacy development through read-aloud, it can influence motivation and development in reading skill. According to Friedman, read-aloud programs that have the greatest impact share the commonality of an advanced reader to mediate the learner's experience (1997). Learners who read and engage with a variety of stories have a greater likelihood of becoming lifelong readers and perform better in multiple measures (Krashen 2004; Ross, McKechnie, and Rothbauer 2006). Read-aloud is packed with positive benefits and can be the cornerstone of many growth experiences.

Reading Aloud: A Brief History

The Oral Tradition

We, as humans, seem to be drawn to the act of reading aloud. Where do the origins of this attraction begin? Storytelling could ultimately be the source, dating back to around 200,000 BCE and the birth of human speech. Storytelling is primal and found in multiple indigenous cultures that predate or coexist with drawn and written societal communication development. We find pattern and comfort in storytelling; it is an ordered way to engage and learn about our chaotic existence. The learning conveyed in early storytelling was packed with practical information that served to sustain humanity (Delistraty 2014; Kluger 2017; Mendoza 2015). The early storytelling shared daily existence, rituals, and events involving the hunt (Big Fish Presentations 2012). Verbal storytelling served the purpose of sharing information needed for human survival and entertainment. The information sharing across time was only as accurate as the storyteller.

The Symbolic Visual Tradition

The symbolic visual tradition started around 30,000 BCE as a precursor to written language and as a method to communicate an idea or message over time. Cave paintings from around 15,000 BCE found in France display excellent examples of this early form of visual storytelling. The cave-drawn images depict multiple animals, round dots, humans, and handprints. A set of Mesopotamian tablets from around 3500 BCE were found entombed in the sheltering Middle Eastern sands safe from the elements. These tablets were covered in 100 key triangular alphabetic symbols needing to be deciphered in order to attain their meaning. The tablets' elusive secrets were only unlocked when approached as a story. This story ultimately became known as *The Epic of Gilgamesh* (Delistraty 2014). The hieroglyphs of ancient Egypt date back to around 2900 BCE and are noted as one of the first alphabetic systems known to humans (Mendoza 2015). The early forms of symbolic communication of ideas helped convey accurate messages over time but were limited in scope and precision of interpretation.

The Written Tradition

Circa 1050 BCE, the first alphabetic language based on sound was developed by the Phoenicians. In China, 305 to 1050 CE, the first printing presses were evolving from relying on wooden blocks to clay as a means of reproduction. In 1450 CE the first newspapers appeared in Europe, followed within five years by the Johannes Gutenberg printing press with movable type. The movement toward mass media proliferation had begun to take shape, giving humanity the ability to replicate and share thoughts via the printed word. This evolution brought about conditions that were favorable for humankind to have increased access to reading materials and ultimately the opportunity to be more literate as a society. The increased level of literacy was still low by modern standards, around 10 to 20 percent. This low level of literacy set the stage for read-aloud's rocky road to the present day.

Reading Aloud Rocks the Ages!

What is it about verbally sharing the written word that resonates so strongly with our internal humanity? Reading aloud is a part of human societal evolution, finding its roots in oral storytelling tradition. During the past 5,000 years of written language, solo reading was a relatively new concept. The Greeks, European monks, and those literate during the Dark Ages always read aloud. Not everyone was literate or in possession of reading materials, so to read aloud was the common practice and helped to share knowledge. Reading aloud strengthened community ties and handed down knowledge between generations. Day commented that during medieval times those who read aloud were revered members of royal courts (2013).

Ultimately, there is human intimacy to the shared read-aloud experience. During the time when reading aloud was a primary form of entertainment, people were able to deliver the stories as ensemble groups in segments and share them over time. Historian Robert Darnton wrote, "For the common people in early modern Europe, reading was a social activity. It took place in workshops, barns, and taverns. It was almost always oral but not necessarily edifying" (Ha 2017). Often there might be rhetorical training for boys, although this was primarily to support the community socially, not for the educational value (Day 2013). Reading aloud was heralded as entertainment, learning, and cultural awareness all in one package. These experiences often included interjecting emotion and theatrics. This form was able to catch nuances of the text that can be lost in silent reading (Day 2013).

Historically, reading has been a communally shared activity. Early texts in Latin were created without spaces between words. Reading aloud facilitated understanding of the written word without spacing. Irish monks, translating Latin, added spaces between words to help them engage the text with greater understanding. Eventually, spaces were routinely added in Latin text to facilitate religious silent reading and reproduction of text in multiple languages. It is hypothesized that a shift in the way words were laid out on a page facilitated the change toward silent reading (Ha 2017).

The Media Tradition

By the 17th century, silent reading was the norm. Through technological advances such as movable type and printing presses like Gutenberg's, contemporary technology began to allow for multiple copies of information. This enabled the sharing of cultural experience and knowledge on a scale never before experienced. The learned and vocal of the day had a plethora of outlets to pursue for dissemination of their words.

During this period, time to read and think alone became possible for the educated wealthy who could afford books. The advent of idle time for rumination was accompanied by an increase in literacy due in part to an increased diversity of genre and range of formats in reading materials. The progression to an array of formats included novels, children's literature, newspapers, and periodicals.

This was the evolution toward the media period. In the 1800s our society viewed the first photographic image, created by Joseph Nicephore Niepce. This photographic accomplishment ushered in the remainder of the 1800s as the era of mass media where inventors such as Alexander Graham Bell and Thomas Edison submitted patents for influential devices like the electric telephone and wax cylinder recording, respectively. The 1900s saw the birth of radio and film, leading to the rise of television in the 1950s. The advancement of the media tradition progressed from multiple copies of written materials to facilitating group learning, to being able to see, hear, and engage with content in a passive firsthand experience.

This gradual development in societal reading habits from social to solitary may have been instrumental in creating the interior life, allowing silent reading and the development of an internal visual world in your head. Silent reading freed readers to explore ideas individually and follow their own curiosity without prying eyes or judgments, allowing dissenting private thought (Saenger 1997).

The cultural shift created from the change to interior reading life cemented our progress toward varied reading materials and cultural literacy. This transition is the subject of argumentative discussion among scholars. If silent reading was rare or rude in ancient times, then at some point the social norm surrounding reading shifted. Today, if we were seated at lunch, in an airport, or at the bus stop, and someone began to read aloud, it would feel like a breach in the social contract. You can read, but do it silently. It seemed like our once-rich read-aloud tradition would be relegated to an experience for only the youngest of us to enjoy.

The Digital Tradition

Technology has impacted our interactions and sharing of societal knowledge. Since the 1800s, photography, radio, motion pictures, telephones, television, digital media, and social media have become hugely influential factors of human existence. Into the age of the interior life came the advancement that would personalize information-seeking behaviors to meet personal desires at the point of need and interest—the Internet.

The modern digital era rose to a crescendo in 1994 with the U.S. government releasing control of the Internet. The World Wide Web was born and changed the speed and style of human information exchange and reading forever, creating a platform that houses all manner of digital media that can be solitarily engaged, explored, and judged for quality and continuing the shift to a more internal existence.

The 21st century has given rise to myriad interactive media platforms such as Facebook, Twitter, Snapchat, and Instagram. These social media platforms allow participants to share information in a variety of media: written word, icons, photos, and video. "This is intriguing because technology has given us the ability to practice our intrinsic nature as visual and verbal individuals" (Mendoza 2015), bringing together all of our traditions under one umbrella. So from cave drawings, to storytelling, to read-aloud, to libraries with eBooks, to app buying, we have hungered through the ages to share our cultural experiences with others and give our society a shared history.

Issues Related to Reading Aloud with Technology

Reading aloud can be a cultural awakening to the shared human connection and a tool for the greater good. We have explored the rich, storied chronicle of the read-aloud. Why with this proven record of success would we want to change the read-aloud to include technology? We have all stood in front of a group to perform and wondered if the experience would successfully engage participants. Would participants be able to connect with the information? Greg Toppo (2015), in the *Atlantic*, interviewed a longtime school librarian, Laura Fleming, noting the changing connection between participants and books.

As a practicing librarian with 12 years of experience, Laura spent time in pursuit of engaging books for read-aloud with her participants. Each year it seemed they became less interested in her offerings. Fleming felt like a comedian performing for students: she stated, "You have that go-to joke that always gets the crowd going" (Toppo 2015, 1). The materials she was selecting and sharing were not capturing her audience. Regardless of her preparation and attempts at engagement, the time came when the books she selected were no longer reaching participants.

So, how did Laura address this? She thought outside the traditional book and engaged participants with the *Skeleton Creek* series that included embedded URLs that augmented the plot. This change brought about greater engagement in the read-aloud material (Toppo 2015). The engagement brought about focus and perhaps spurred learning as well within the read-aloud process.

Laura stated that *Inanimate Alice* is a book her participants enjoyed through digital read-alouds. The lines between books and other media are blurred for her participants. They do not see the distinction between traditional books and transmedia materials; they see all as information sources. "*Alice's* world, she said, is the world kids are growing up in" (Toppo 2015, 1). For better or for worse, digitally augmented books are a part of our personal, professional, and educational landscapes (Paganelli 2016). Into this digital read-aloud terrain we seek to successfully incorporate technology. This can be a daunting process. What are the challenging issues surrounding the incorporation of technology to create digital read-aloud experiences for our participants?

Read-aloud is found to be accomplished on a daily basis by less than half of classroom teachers. Seventy-six percent of teachers do not plan for read-aloud. Even our youngest children may not be involved in read-aloud on a daily basis. The typical read-aloud includes an adult reading from a trade book for 10–20 minutes. Literature is on average not curriculum integrated, and the amount of discussion is less than five minutes. The current read-aloud is traditionally lacking in technology. We are potentially missing a multitude of opportunities for participant growth, and we are not maximizing technology impact opportunities.

Are all read-alouds created equal? No, the read-aloud experience can have levels of quality and benchmarks of success. Based on research, a successful read-aloud will show the following traits:

- Reading aloud is frequent or regular.
- Participant choice/voice is present.

- Leaders select quality multimedia information.

- Leaders share literature related to other literature.

- The read-aloud makes time for quality, thoughtful discussion.

- Participants are grouped for greatest impact on experience.

- Leaders offer a variety of extension opportunities.

- Multiple response opportunities are offered.

- Leaders reread selected books/passages: don't be afraid to repeat, repeat, repeat yourself (Hoffman, Roser, and Battle 1993).

- Leaders include technology to maximize connection and impact with digital-age learner participants.

To these quality elements we are going to add technology to create the digital read-aloud. We will power up our read-alouds by building reading excitement through technology. The quest toward inclusion of technology in the read-aloud experience is not without its challenges. The following issues will help us frame our discussion of challenges and ultimately how to overcome them: "To tech or not to tech?" "What is a book anyway?" "What is reading anyway?" and "What is appropriate use of technology in the read-aloud?"

Issue One: To Tech or Not to Tech?

That is not the question. We all use technology. Technology is neither good nor evil. Technology is a tool that can serve many purposes and bolster success. Technology use is a life skill that can be shared as value-added in the read-aloud experience. Still, some are resistant to the incorporation of technology into the read-aloud experience, as shown in Figure 1.1. This is in part due to the archetype of the read-aloud that has its origin in childhood.

Reading aloud is usually represented as an adult reading to a child seated with a book. The read-aloud archetype usually doesn't differ greatly from our first experiences with read-aloud, which is generally shared first with a single adult (typically a parent or guardian), then with a small group (cultural, social activity) and eventually in a classroom setting. The read-aloud archetype consists of an advanced reader, selected literature, and seating in a quiet area. A change in this formula can cause discomfort in primarily predigital age adult read-aloud facilitators. Education, training, and library occupation professionals have a median age of 42.7 (Data USA 2016). According to the Schools and Staffing Survey the average teacher age is 42 (NCES 2012). Individuals in this age range are generally considered predigital. Many predigitals do not feel as comfortable sharing knowledge through technology. This can mean that the read-aloud participant experience for those served by the predigital population is technology-free.

Mount Pearl Public Library (Ross King Memorial)
September 29, 2015 ·

Like Page

This is a new banner that our sister library in Churchill Falls had made! LOVE IT!

Wowzers! This post has really taken off and we would love to credit the lady who came up with this slogan. Ms. Kim Bonnell is Vice-Chair of the Churchill Falls Library board and a grade 2 teacher. Kim would like everyone to use this freely and- of course- read to your child!

Figure 1.1   Using an app to say there is no app to replace the lap! Read to your child. Why does it have to be one way or the other? Can't the two experiences successfully combine?

Issue Two: What Is a Book Anyway?

Does read-aloud imply a traditional book? No, a book can be in many formats. The traditional book is plucked from the shelf and opened via a cover, hinging on the spine to reveal pages. These pages are then read in a mostly linear fashion, and the story is followed to its conclusion. The traditional book can be seen in many incarnations:

- Picture books: typically around 25 pages in length. Large in size with multiple images.
- Wordless books: no words at all; pictures tell the story.
- Emergent readers: smaller and have more words, fewer pictures than a true picture book.
- Chapter books: this is the common term for fiction with fewer illustrations as the reading level increases.

- Graphic novel: story told in a comic book format.
- Novel in verse: a novel written in free verse style.
- Story in rhyme: the story is told using a rhyme scheme.
- Hardcover: the book is jacketed in a rigid cover.
- Paperback: the book is jacketed in a flexible covering.

The transmedia eBook takes the above-listed aspects of the traditional book and pulls them into myriad digital formats. The transmedia eBook experience integrates animations that add to the story, aid comprehension, and improve the visual experience when contrasted with traditional books' illustrations. Transmedia eBooks can be downloaded and read on eReaders that can mimic the tactile practice of turning pages. Transmedia eBooks can reach the digital native generation of readers who are not wedded to the idea of traditional books as nondigital natives are; to them, information is information and the form of delivery is secondary (Roslund 2012).

Our students recognize information in all its formats; they do not recognize a book in the same way we do. The line in our culture between books and multimedia has blurred. We struggle to define the variations. So for the purposes of our discussion, we will call all our versions of text transmedia (although the Franken novel was a distant but cool second place) (Toppo 2015).

Luckily, transmedia done right does exist! The facilitator selections need to be deliberate to aid us in finding the right fit, using in part the guidelines listed below. This can open up many options for read-aloud delivery. To meet the following criteria, the transmedia information must have quality of topic, narration, writing, and format.

- Is the content of literary quality?
- Is it user-friendly?
- Is the narration well done and engaging?
- Does the narration allow for pausing to engage the story and ask questions?
- Do multiple sensory modalities impact the effectiveness of information (Roslund 2012)?

Issue Three: What Is Reading Anyway?

But aren't we reading when on technology and social media? Yes, but it is impacting our learning in an unexpected way. Is the exposure to transmedia material changing the manner in which we learn to read? Daniel Willingham states that the cognitive processes by which we learn to read aren't changing with the advent of technology. In terms of total amount of words encountered we are reading more than ever, thanks in part to text messaging. Willingham believes that our reading habits are adjusting over time to match technology. Ours is a complicated learning environment; much of the online interaction that takes place involves reading, including texting, social media, and even gaming. That increases word knowledge and exposure. However, the increased exposure does not necessarily mean greater skill. Reading comprehension will not be impacted due to this exposure (Korbey 2018; Trelease 2006). The implementation of digital read-aloud on a deliberate path toward reading competency should be our focus. Planning the use of quality transmedia could have a strong impact when children's books contain 50 percent more rare words than other media formats (Duursma, Augustyn, and Zuckerman 2008).

Issue Four: What Is Appropriate Use of Technology in the Read-Aloud?

Technology used appropriately can support learning and enhance cognitive and social abilities. A focus on active, engaged use rather than passive is beneficial (Campbell and Hansen 2014). According to a 2010 study, eBooks are helpful in assisting with reading comprehension but are most effective in conjunction with the presence of a more advanced reader. Why is having an advanced reader supporting and modeling beginning transmedia reading experiences so important? Reading online changes attention; the pressing issue is how reading online complicates the comprehension process. As more and more of kids' reading takes place online, research shows that reading online requires greater attention than reading a traditional book. Many technology-enriched reading experiences offer multiple choices, requiring attention to know when to return to the text narrative. It is easy to become distracted by the sometimes nonlinear nature of transmedia materials (Korbey 2018). Advanced reader adult guidance will aid our participants in navigating the opportunities for learning present in transmedia.

The Importance of Technology Inclusion in Read-Aloud

Use of technology to support learning development is an embattled topic worth addressing. Julie Atkinson's son grabs the iPad and settles into bed for some reading time through a kids' book app. Atkinson, who guesses that her family of four spends half their reading time with physical books, said that she has noticed a difference between how her son reads paper books and how he reads digitally. He has a tendency to skim more in apps and move more rapidly through the offered materials (Korbey 2018).

We are read aloud to as children, but that drops off as we grow older. This is felt keenly in the transition between third and fourth grade. It is commonly known that we transition from exclusively learning to read toward reading to learn. This process can create an experience for learners called the "fourth-grade slump." The fourth-grade slump has affected many students adversely and created some learners who are resistant readers. This phenomenon could be addressed by the continuation of read-aloud with the incorporation of technology and an advanced reader facilitator to meet participants at the point of need.

We as advanced reader facilitators in the read-aloud experience have a responsibility to spread our cultural knowledge through read-aloud. To make the sharing of cultural knowledge have the most impact, it should be positive to engage students where they feel most comfort, in the digital world. To begin, having insightful understanding of our participants' views on books, information, media, and technology as equal and integral to each other would be beneficial. Regardless of the format, our participants need positive experiences with lots of books in an environment that encourages lifelong learning under the supervision or a trained facilitator, who can bring joy and interest into reading (Atwell 2007). Technology is ubiquitous. Read-alouds are, however, predominately lacking in technology. Should we care?

Conclusion

"It seemed to tap into something—a kind of long-forgotten tradition that we still felt in our bones. Reading aloud has a noble history" (Day 2013). How has the advent of social technology impacted the interior life of our culture? It has long been thought that the advent of the printing press heralded the end to reading aloud for pleasure outside of the children's educational environment. However, research does not entirely support that idea. Reading is a pleasure-centered accrued skill. The more you read, the better a reader you become. Encouraging pleasure in reading encourages growth in reading skills. Reading aloud for pleasure has maintained popularity in multiple formats (Chisholm 2017), though one could guess that reading aloud for pleasure would become rare when supplanted by more visually engaging media.

Adults are not using technology to communicate societal knowledge in the same way the oral storytelling tradition did. How can we encourage this sharing of knowledge? Technology infused read-aloud could be a way to meet our youth where they are in the digital world. Everyone should be an advocate for reading aloud, and the proper use of technology is a life skill. This advocacy for the appropriate use of technology during reading aloud will serve to support the learning and engagement of all participants, changing the way we experience read-aloud. This book is not about teaching participants to read; it is about engaging them with an advanced reader facilitator, technology, and quality transmedia literature so they want to be better readers and obtain information—and in the process create lifelong learners.

No one tells us what to do when the books we have loved and shared verbally with countless others begin to be received with a chilly reception. This experience has left some feeling like an entertainer bombing at delivery while the only sound is crickets chirping (Toppo 2015). When the verbal no longer reaches participants, it may be time to incorporate the visual. In these cases the "app isn't replacing the book; it's showing you a way to bridge the gap between the old and the new" (Thorne 2012).

The eBook is not a replacement; it is an augmentation to the experience. We can acknowledge, respect, and understand our history with read-aloud while building a bridge to a digitally enhanced world of learning and meet our students at the point of need. Get your digital transmedia information and technologies ready, people. It is on! Everyone should be an advocate for reading-aloud with technology.

CHAPTER TWO

Knowing Your Audience Is Key to Planning for Digital Read-Aloud

Could facilitator modeling of screen time technology use be a part of the societal good that is read-aloud?

Reading aloud is viewed as a panacea for all our reading ills. If you wish your participants to have a greater vocabulary, read to them. If you wish your participants to possess greater comprehension skills, read to them. Reading aloud to participants can be the answer to many concerns.

Readers experience danger zones of drop-off at the three skill levels: basic, proficient, and advanced. Most children learn to read by fourth grade, but the progression then stalls, and by eighth grade, 24 percent are below basic level and 42 percent are at basic, with 25 percent at proficient and 3 percent at advanced. To combat this fourth-grade slump in which the readers thrive and the strugglers are challenged to succeed, we need to connect reading with pleasure—reading is an accrued skill that we need to practice consistently (Trelease 2013).

Our participants, according to the Kaiser Foundation's longitudinal study, are societal screen time technology users at the rate of at least six or more hours a day for those up to age 10. Screen time technology use increases with age and tops out with 18 year olds at as much as 11 hours a day. Our youth aged 8 to 18 years average 8 hours of technology use on a typical day. This averages out to be around 56 hours a week. Much of this time is spent multitasking on more than one medium at a time. They can actually manage to pack more than 10 hours of additional media content into those original

8 hours through the use of multiscreen multitasking. The amount of time spent with technology has been snowballing (HKFF 2010).

These statistics are alarming and compounded by technology use being primarily passive and outside of the educational realm (HKFF 2010). The ease of 24-hour access to entertainment media has served to increase the amount of time children and teens are engaging with technology. Our generation of 8- to 18-year-olds has access to multiscreen media via iPads and cell phones, enabling ease of use. Since 2004, Americans who are 8 to 18 years old have had an uptick from 39 to 66 percent in their ownership of mobile media devices. This one-to-one engagement has led to increased music listening, playing games, watching television, and talking on the phone.

Only about 3 in 10 young people say they have rules about how much time they can spend watching TV and playing video games, and they say the same about using the computer. But when limits are set, less time is spent with multiscreen media—nearly three hours fewer per day. About two-thirds say the television is frequently on during meals, and half say the TV is left on in their home, even if no one is watching. Seven out of ten have a television in their bedroom, and half have a video game console in their room (HKFF 2010).

Drew Altman states, "The amount of time young people spend with media has grown to where it's even more than a full-time work week. When we are spending this much time doing anything, we need to understand how it's affecting us—for good and bad" (HKFF 2010). Those of our participants who use more technology usually have lower grades (HKFF 2010). A causal effect cannot be drawn, but if you spend the equivalent of a full-time job on multiscreen technology, in passive use mode, it is logical it will impact your learning—for good and bad.

As the proliferation of technology continues to bolster participant use, the research on how that technology is used continues to grow in importance. Our participants are engaging in high levels of multiscreen media multitasking (HKFF 2010). How this impacts engagement in other areas is a source of curiosity and concern. The following points from research generated by the Henry J. Kaiser Family Foundation offer some context:

- About half of 8- to 18-year-olds say they use multiscreen media either most or some of the time they're doing their homework.

- Fewer than half of all 8- to 18-year-olds say they have rules about what and when they can engage with technology.

- There are substantial differences in multiscreen media use between members of various ethnic and racial groups.

- Girls spend more time than boys using social media, listening to music, and reading. Boys spend more time than girls playing console video games, computer games, and going to video websites like YouTube.

- Multiscreen media use increases when children hit the 11–14-year-old age group, an increase to almost 12 hours per day.
- Seventh to twelfth graders report spending an average of two hours per day sending or receiving texts.
- Over the past five years, time spent reading books remained steady at about 25 minutes a day (HKFF 2010).

In a world of technology proliferation, people who will participate in our read-alouds engage in multiscreen media technology use for 56 hours and spend less than 3 hours per week in dedicated reading time. Does the pre-digital read-aloud experience optimally engage the tech-savvy digital native? We need to make the digital read-aloud experience part of those 56 hours in order to meet participants where they live, in the digital world. Our digital natives have a changing connection, relationship, and definition of "book." During a recent conference presentation, an educator commented that when asking how summer technology screen time was spent, the responses were computer gaming, television, iPad, iPod, and music to differing degrees, but all of the students engaged in YouTube. Our participants are coming to us with a vast experience of information sharing from a multitude of YouTube personalities on a plethora of topics. The experiences of the read-aloud and screen time technology use of "YouTube story time" are alien to one another, but they don't need to be. The aims are drastically different, but using technology for engagement could become a commonality. We can build a bridge between quality transmedia literature and productive screen time technology use to power up our existing read-alouds, building reading excitement through technology.

Using Technology-Infused Digital Read-Aloud to Augment Engagement

We have all stood in front of a group to perform a read-aloud and wondered if our information would successfully capture the participants' attention. Would participants be able to connect with the material? Greg Toppo, in *The Atlantic*, interviewed a longtime school librarian who noted the changing connection between students and books. Regardless of her preparation and attempts at engagement, the time came when the books she selected were no longer reaching participants (Toppo 2015, 1). She turned to transmedia.

"It was, she remembered, the first standing ovation she ever received as a librarian" (Toppo 2015, 1). The addition of digital transmedia aspects to read-aloud had created an environment of excitement, revitalizing interest. The standing ovation was due to reading aloud a series of young adult novels called *Skeleton Creek* that contained URL links to a series of gritty "*Blair Witch*-style videos," which appear to be shot by the character. What this offered was an increased amount of multimodal participant engagement.

She later used *Inanimate Alice*, a multiple media digital book, and engaged her participants in a way they had never before experienced. She was able to use pictures, sound, and text in an online format to grab students' attention. The read-and-click-forward format was similar to page turning but supported with many visual and auditory elements. Their excitement was palpable; after she projected the story onto the whiteboard the participants were hooked. "A few students approached her afterwards to thank her, tears glistening in their eyes" (Toppo 2015, 1). The immersive possibilities for engagement create an opportunity to influence participants of all ages (Paganelli 2016)!

The advanced reader facilitator-guided digital read-aloud experience could be the model for appropriate engagement with transmedia that our participants lack with other multiscreen formats of technology interaction. Students participate in topics they wish to explore or ideas they find intriguing. Connecting with the idea at the beginning of the theme builds excitement for the digital read-aloud that is to come.

Digital Read-Aloud Can Be Used to Promote Lifelong Learning in Varied Ages and Demographics

Excitement, innovation, and engagement can come from powered-up digital read-aloud at any age. Our participant audience for the digital read-aloud experience could include all of the following: children, tweens, teens, young adults, adults, the middle-aged, seniors, singles, couples, married people, parents, siblings, grandparents, caregivers, people in all lifetime stages, and all socioeconomic factors, orientations, ethnicities, and gender identifications in between. The demographics for read-aloud experiences are continually becoming more diverse. In 1984 one in four school-aged children were considered a minority. In 2020 it is projected to be one in two students who are considered a minority. School-aged children with special needs are also on the rise. Some of the participant populations in the digital read-aloud may require support to have an equitable shared experience. These populations include but are not limited to the following:

- Mental disabilities
- Learning disabilities
- Emotional disabilities
- Physical disabilities (visual, auditory, and mobility)
- Chronic illnesses
- Attention deficit disorders
- At-risk backgrounds
- Transient family backgrounds (migrant or homeless) (Bishop and Cahall 2012)

In order to know your participant audience is receiving an equitable digital read-aloud experience, it is important to consider the following areas: demographics, disposition, and knowledge. The listed inquiries can be used in full or in part as necessary. The inquiry can be formal or informal depending on your ability to obtain information prior to implementing the digital read-aloud. The questioning can also be done immediately prior to implementation through quick questioning with verbal, physical, or virtual response. The analysis of demographics may consist of the following areas as appropriate and deemed necessary:

What is the average age of my participants?

- What range of ages is represented?
- Does this range include generational overlap?
- Does the age impact an overlap of interest or a disparity of interest?

Is my reading audience homogeneous or heterogeneous?

- If homogeneous, how are the participants alike?
- What do they have in common?
- If heterogeneous, how are the participants different from one another?
- What do participants have in common despite their differences?

In terms of socioeconomic status, how would I describe my participant audience?

- Where do they fit in society's social and economic status?
- Why does this matter and should it be addressed?
- What occupations are represented in my participant audience?
- What are my participants' political and religious affiliations?
- What ethnic, racial, and cultural groups are represented in my participant audience?
- What is my role in relationship to my participant audience?
- How can I connect with my participants?

The analysis of disposition may include the following;

- What might my participant audience expect from this experience?
- What might I expect about my participants' attitudes toward me (the facilitator) and my topic?
- What concerns or problems do my participants have?
- What interests and goals do my participants have?

- What will motivate my participants?
- What types of needs do they have?
- What biases or preconceived ideas might my participants have about me (the facilitator) and the topic?

The use of knowledge analysis can benefit the participants in read-aloud by analyzing:

- How much does my participant audience already know about my topic?
- What can I inform my participants about that they do not already know?
- What new information would my participants benefit from?
- How could they use this new transmedia information?
- At what point of sophistication will I be "talking over the heads" of my participant audience because my transmedia information is too complex?
- At what point of sophistication will I be "insulting the intelligence" of my participant audience because my transmedia information is too simplistic?
- What questions might my participants have about my topic or ideas (Kagan 2018)?

Yes, we can care and make a difference in the shared digital read-aloud experience of our diverse participant audience through deliberate planning, consideration, respect, and recognition of similarities and differences—by providing equity. In a world of technology proliferation, does the predigital read-aloud experience optimally engage the potentially diverse technology-savvy participant? Digital read-aloud is a simple concept that can have a complex delivery capable of serving all of society no matter the age, ethnicity, gender, socioeconomic level, or technology knowledge of our participants.

For participants who are English-language learners, there are opportunities for rich cross-cultural sharing. Supporting advanced activities, along with attention to idioms, multiple-meaning words, textual clues, pictures, and various grouping configurations, assists all students in participating with the class. Facilitators may also support acquiring English by providing careful modeling, demonstrations, and scaffolding, and by having reading materials available at various levels of difficulty and transmedia format. Opportunities for a variety of response methods support involvement. Encourage those acquiring English to participate in group activities and motivate them to engage in language learning sharing (Vogt 1997).

Digital Read-Aloud Can Be Used One-on-One, in Small Groups, or for Many

Digital read-aloud can support a multimethod learning environment effectively, including one-on-one, small groups, and large groups. In the context of deliberate grouping, the digital read-aloud experience can allow for a multitude of personalized learning practices meeting participants at the point of need. The choices made by facilitators can aid the impact of digital read-aloud on individual participant experience and success. Let us group participants for optimal opportunities to respond and to participate fully. Attention to group size can provide greater participant comfort and allow for discussions that impact participant experience (Hoffman, Roser, and Battle 1993).

How can participants learn effectively in one-on-one, small group, and large group read-aloud environments? Careful, deliberate planning with flexibility can be our most effective tool in any participant organizational pattern. For participants, it allows for a variety of approaches to meet their needs. For facilitators it allows for configurations to maximize impact on participant experience and serve needs more strategically (Vogt 1997).

One-on-one opportunities provide for participants to engage personally with an advanced reader facilitator or participant. Transmedia reading aloud to the participant can be accomplished through shared or participant partner reading (Duursma, Augustyn, and Zuckerman 2008). Participants are given time for self-selected reading and activities to include participant choice and allow for increased voice.

Small group read-aloud has the advantage of variety because of its use of multiple small grouping configurations. Participants may work together in cooperative learning groups of four or more. At other times, however, participants may want to work in smaller triads for a more intimate learning experience. Grouping decisions may be made jointly by the facilitator and participants based on which configuration might be the best for any particular activity or participant audience.

The traditional large group configuration for some activities is efficient and appropriate. It provides the most direct route to read-aloud information delivery and allows for the greatest amount of communal group experience.

Digital Read-Aloud Can Be Cross-Curricular and Embrace Any Subject

Cross-curricular instruction is defined as "a conscious effort to apply knowledge, principles, and/or values to more than one academic discipline simultaneously. The disciplines may be related through a central theme, issue, problem, process, topic, or experience" (Harb 2007). Participants can be encouraged to engage in cross-curricular digital read-aloud by engaging their emergent interests in certain topics or ideas. Authentic participant-driven topics can come from a focus on participants' interests and extend beyond ideas into reality, involving a variety of interactive media opportunities; creating opportunity for discussion and collaboration; and building on participant background knowledge, skills, aptitude, and language. Cross-curricular topics integrate literature across content areas, such as language arts, math, science, history, social studies, and visual performing arts.

Those considered to be good readers make connections with topics and ideas from a variety of previous life experiences (Anderson et al. 1985). Sustained attentive reading improves skill apprehension and enhances enjoyment; over time this practice improves comprehension. To encourage this practice, access to a variety of transmedia materials—narrative, expository, and informational—is essential. This variety allows for a framework of knowledge to be laid that will prepare us to integrate what we have learned in a manner engaging cross-curricular topics and ideas (Vogt 1997).

Topical instruction can acquire, communicate, and investigate worthwhile knowledge in depth. Participants come to think of cross-curricular content areas as connected, rather than isolated, because content areas are studied within the context of an authentic topic or idea. Active exploration of an authentic topic promotes integration and enrichment of language processes. Cross-curricular instruction can encourage information engagement using different kinds of transmedia materials with a variety of screen-based delivery methods as displayed in Figure 2.1.

Building on current knowledge, prior knowledge, past knowledge, and experiences of the world, participants create relationships among various sources of transmedia information. As new ideas are formed, they become integrated with previously learned information. The participant audience is able to make choices and explore authentic topics of interest, placing relevance contextually. The participant audience is invited to make choices based on their interests, abilities, and needs while applying what they learn in meaningful and authentic real-world contexts. As participants explore topics

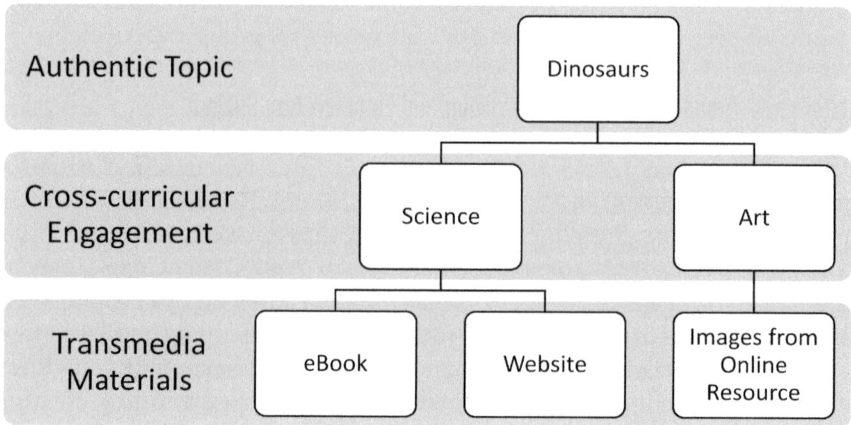

Figure 2.1   Outline of the process of authentic topic exploration.

through a variety of transmedia information source materials, they learn to relate what they are learning to their own lives. Activities for home exploration help participants bridge cross-curricular content learning, with the intent of developing problem-solving and decision-making skills (Vogt 1997).

Cross-curricular learning can meet the needs of many and encourage learning, regardless of demographics, disposition, and knowledge. One advantage of cross- curricular read-aloud is that it is both flexible and adaptable. Because a variety of informational transmedia materials are utilized, all have the opportunity to address interest at the appropriate challenge level. Cross-curricular read-aloud can support a multimethod learning environment effectively, including diverse, multiage participants configured as individuals, in small groups or in large groups.

Helping *all* participants succeed requires support for those struggling with rigor, topic, technology, and reading skill. In other more traditional read-aloud formats, those who struggled to engage were frequently included as passive participants and practiced self-selected exclusion from questioning and other activities that could lead to exploration, discovery, and critical thinking. Cross-curricular digital read-aloud has the potential to foster full participant inclusion, personalization of the learning process, and participant engagement.

The personalization of learning experience is desired whether an activity is more effective with large group, small group, or individual instruction. Depending on the difficulty of the reading selection, the nature of the activity, and, of course, the abilities and interests of the participants, the personalization will vary. Participant input can be captured and utilized; most want more control over their learning.

In order to capture and utilize input and knowledge we will encourage participant agency. So . . . what is participant agency, and why is it important to our practice as read-aloud facilitators? Participant agency encompasses multiple areas of interest, such as interaction between participant and personalized learning technology, working toward creating self-reliant learners, and empowering participants to take control of their own learning.

The concept of participant agency can be defined simply as the ability to take ownership of personal learning. Agency, according to Eric Toshalis and Michael J. Nakkula (2012), is comprised of motivation, engagement, and voice. This three-pronged approach comprises the lens that will focus this discussion of participant agency.

Motivation doesn't stand alone; it exists in an ever-changing environment that is dependent on our experiences. Intelligence is dynamic; this knowledge should be a part of the participant experience along with opportunities for praise, self-determination, and feedback. Each of our participants will have a personally unique path toward setting and achieving goals. To support our participants, we need to become the experts in their learning processes and customize the digital read-aloud experience to meet them at the point of need.

Engagement has four areas of emphasis: (1) attention engagement (time on task, activities attempted), (2) behavioral engagement (attendance, participation, questioning), (3) cognitive engagement (self-regulation, learning goals, and perceived relevance), and (4) psychological engagement (feelings of identification or belonging, relationships, personal independence). When participants are engaged, they will see benefit in their digital read-aloud experiences and feel the value and ownership of the space and program.

Participant voice can be understood as the communication and influence in co-constructing the digital read-aloud environment. Voice is the expression of allowing participants profound impact in the environment and their learning. This can be the most challenging, provocative, and rewarding aspect of participant agency. It has the potential to be personal and speaks to the heart of the art and science of our learner practice.

In truth, we work hard to convince participants that read-aloud is worth their attention, time, and effort. We are encouraged to cultivate tasks and experiences that support critical thinkers and makers. The movement to create critical thinkers and makers could benefit from an understanding that participant agency and transmedia in the digital read-aloud can foster these skills and many other immeasurable impacts (Rosenthal and Boser 2012).

How can we begin to give participants control of their learner experience in the digital read-aloud? Developing a culture of participant agency in the digital read-aloud can be accomplished in many ways. One means is a passionate call to action through advocacy, encouraging participant control of their learning with strategic facilitator guidance in the form of story author or code author experiences. Capitalizing on this initial engagement can create greater opportunities for participants to explore their own agency as they play and develop effective strategies and habits of mind. This is an excellent and timely vehicle for an in-depth look at participant voice and linking personal interests to digital read-aloud learning.

There's a movement toward really engaging learners individually to activate engagement, motivation, and voice. The idea behind student voice and student agency is that participants can take control of facets of their own learning—isn't it liberating to think that we could give that to participants? I want my participants to have it, and every learner I know wants all of us to have that.

Cross-curricular digital read-aloud allows participants to reflect the world as they know it, explore, and discover, thus expressing their agency. Culminating with the activity in which transmedia information has been used, or final sharing as a work product, enriches the experience, encouraging lifelong learning as illustrated in Figure 2.2. The common link in the digital read-aloud learning is transmedia information connected to the world from which we branch out and investigate (Vogt 1997).

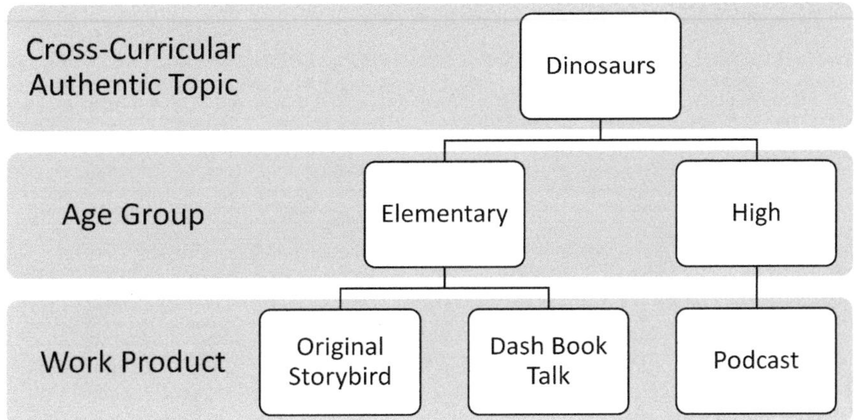

Figure 2.2   Outline of the process of authentic topic exploration.

Conclusion

Fluency is a building process; success in reading at ages six and seven is cultivated through knowledge gleaned from experiences at ages three to five, such as exposure to alliteration and rhyme transmitted through quality literature (Duursma, Augustyn, and Zuckerman 2008). Preschoolers are learning to draw conclusions between the spoken and written word through the use of alliteration and rhyme; reading aloud encourages the development of skills that can translate to earlier success in reading (Duursma, Augustyn, and Zuckerman 2008). The U.S. Department of Education commissioned a study on reading; two of the major findings were that reading aloud provided skills that eventually lead to reading and that this practice should be for all ages at school and at home (Anderson et al. 1985). The call is clear; plan cross-curricular digital read-aloud using transmedia that can engage participants early in development and encourage a lifelong love of reading that links technology and reading in a research-based best practice process of implementation.

CHAPTER THREE

Planning for a Digital Read-Aloud

Yes! It is possible for digital read-aloud to retain important aspects of traditional read-aloud while embracing elements of screen time transmedia technology and engaging our participant audience cross-curricularly.

The mindful and deliberate consideration of participants' demographics, needs, interests, and desires, together with the use of cross-curricular methods and thoughtfully selected transmedia technology and inspired grouping during the digital read-aloud, can set the stage for an experience that will truly meet the needs of learners. When these areas have been addressed, the selection of transmedia information for the digital read-aloud can begin in the categories of augmented reality, dynamic dialogue, story author, and code author.

Digital Resource Type Categories Available for Digital Read-Aloud

Digital read-aloud is a technology-augmented transmedia experience. The mindful and deliberate recognition of the interplay between cherished traditional and captivating new digital read-aloud possibilities is the goal. This can be accomplished through a planning process that focuses on identification of age level, group size, demographics, subject, and transmedia resources.

- Digital read-aloud can be used to promote lifelong learning in varied ages. From our youngest Pre-Ks to our soon-to-be graduates, digital read-aloud can be a tool for learning engagement.

- Digital read-aloud can be used one-on-one, in a small group, or for many. The digital read-aloud experience can allow for personal learning or varied-size group experiences.

- Digital read-aloud can be cross-curricular and embrace any subject. Our call to cross-curricular engagement can be explored within digital read-aloud.

The transmedia resource type categories are augmented reality, dynamic dialogue, story author, and code author formats. Each of these transmedia categories delivers media in a distinct manner. The categories are outlined below with definitions and examples designed to build excitement and power up your imagination and forward incorporation goals in the digital read-aloud. See Table 3.1 for this information in tabular form.

Augmented Reality

Augmented reality makes use of book materials that are standalone while incorporating materials that are digital. This is a hybrid book and application that augments reality and will keep participants' interest (Thorne 2012). A brilliant example is the book and application combination of *The Fantastic Flying Books of Mr. Morris Lessmore* by William Joyce. The book can be shared as a traditional read-aloud or as an augmented reality digital read-aloud.

In a world of augmented reality, it's not a book, not a movie. It can be shared as a projected whiteboard experience. Those skeptical about the storytelling power of technology will be excited by augmented reality. "The app isn't replacing the book; it's showing you a way to bridge the gap between the old and the new," explains Brandon Oldenburg of the company Moonbot that created *The Fantastic Flying Books of Mr. Morris Lessmore* (Thorne 2012, 1). The limitation is that for the book to be truly interactive, each child would need a copy of the text and an iPad.

Dynamic Dialogue

Dynamic dialogue consists of materials that contain embedded audio, dictionary, or other digital functions. The dynamic dialogue can add educational value to the experience by allowing participants to access additional information, audio, visuals, and dictionaries to extend the transmedia learning experience.

From read-aloud to digital read-aloud, eBooks with dynamic dialogue can be used to expand read-aloud and add an element of engagement. Amy Koester spoke of the challenge and excitement in her blog: "I was amazed to see how effectively we can engage an audience with a book app. I realized that the presentation style and level of audience involvement isn't necessarily any

Table 3.1 Examples of Augmented Reality, Dynamic Dialogue, Story Author, and Code Author, Including Title, Author, Format, Age Level, Facilitator Role, Participant Experience, and Cost

Resource Type Category	Title/Author	Format/Age	Facilitator Role	Participant Experience	Cost
Augmented Reality	*The Fantastic Flying Books of Mr. Morris Lessmore,* William Joyce http://moonbot studios.com	Book with Application 4–8	The facilitator will be delivering the traditional book while simultaneously monitoring student iPad use with the accompanying application.	Our participants will experience the best of both worlds with this Augmented Reality inspired session. The experience could be varied based on technology availability. If your library has a single iPad and projection, it can be experienced as a group. If your library has access to a classroom set of iPads, it could be a school library media specialist led personalized learning experience.	Under $20.00
Dynamic Dialogue	*The Going to Bed Book,* Sandra Boynton http://loudcrow .com/the-going -to-bed-book	Application 2–5	The facilitator could be delivering the traditional book or monitoring while modeling student iPad use with the accompanying application with the smart board.	Our participants will enjoy an experience that brings the book to life with interactive elements. The experience could be varied based on technology availability. If your library has a single iPad and projection, it can be experienced as a group. If your library has a few iPads, it could be experienced as small groups. If your library has access to a classroom set of iPads, it could be a school library media specialist led personalized learning experience.	Under $10.00

(continued)

Table 3.1 (*continued*)

Resource Type Category	Title/Author	Format/Age	Facilitator Role	Participant Experience	Cost
Story Author	Storybird Your Students www.storybird .com	Application All Ages	The facilitator role will be one of mentor over student creative progress. This would be a project to lead student creativity and engagement with the Storybird application as students create their own stories.	Our participants will engage in an experience that encourages students to create their own stories. The experience could be varied based on technology availability. If your library has a single iPad and projection, it can be experienced as a group where students are able to create pages together. If your library has a few iPads, it could be experienced as small groups, where students collaboratively create stories. If your library has access to a classroom set of iPads, it can be a personalized learning experience.	Free
Code Author	Dash & Dot Wonder Workshop https://www .makewonder .com	Robots and Application Options	The facilitator role will be one of mentor over student creative progress. This would be a project to lead student creativity and engagement with the Storybird application as students create their own stories.	Our participants will engage in coding robots to act out personal or author written stories. The experience could be varied based on technology availability. If your library has a single robot with application, it can be experienced as small groups, where students collaboratively create code to express stories. If your library has access to a classroom set of robots and iPads, it can be a personalized learning experience.	Robots have varied prices. Applications are free.

different from 'traditional' read-aloud, it's just that the book is so much more visible" (Tran 2014, 1).

Story Author

Story author embraces project-based tools and selected digital objects to create their own original children's books to engage during digital read-aloud. Read-aloud no longer needs to be passive; participants can create and share their own stories for and with classmates.

Participants can have a voice and share their original vision and story. In a digital read-aloud experience near you, participants can create and publish their own eBooks. The participants create their own media that will allow participants to create and share their own books during read-aloud.

Code Author

Code author embraces project-based tools and selected digital objects to allow readers to create and share their own stories through the use of coding. Coding is an important skill to teach kids. Texas has passed legislation to recognize computer science as a second language (Adam 2013). Coding is the difference between our participants reading webpages and creating webpages!

The trend to teach participants coding is augmented by Dot and Dash, robots created by the folks at Wonder Workshop. Dot and Dash are coding robots designed to allow the basics of coding to be learned with ease while myriad other cross-curricular topics are being addressed through digital read-aloud. The robots are equipped with recorded audio and sense each other's presence. Participants can use this to code Dot and Dash to tell an existing or created story. In this way Dot and Dash are able to potentially be the facilitator of the digital read-aloud (while looking adorable) (Paganelli 2016).

Transmedia Resource Selection Process for Digital Read-Aloud

The transmedia resource selection process should mirror the traditional read-aloud method with a bent toward the inclusion of screen time technology. The more traditional elements are listed below:

- Selections should include a wide variety of multiscreen delivery formats and transmedia to engage participants. The original focus on variety of genre has been expanded to include variety of transmedia.
- Selections should be age appropriate and aligned with the technology proficiency of the participants. The original focus on age appropriateness of the

text has been extended to include consideration of the participants' multi-screen technology proficiency.

- Listening levels and engagement levels are different. The listening levels of material can be stretched to include the engagement levels that our participants have with multiple transmedia.

- Selected materials should engage participants. The book selection for engagement has been extended to encompass all materials.

- Selected materials should themselves be extending the digital read-aloud with cross-curricular elements. The selection of materials toward cross-curricular arrangement can allow for a more global experience. To achieve this, it would be positive to engage the bounty of nonfiction materials available in our digital read-aloud experiences (Paganelli 2016; Trelease 2013).

Are we ready to do our digital read-aloud yet? Not quite; more and more researchers state that there is overwhelming evidence that some eBooks are helpful with reading comprehension, but it is time to focus on how functions assist in learning and how often those functions occur in digital transmedia (Roslund 2012).

Digital-age participants don't see the lines between the types of transmedia. It is all seen as information, and multiscreen delivery systems are just different ways to consume it (Campbell and Hansen 2014). Deliberate material selections that require transmedia text quality with supportive technologies can help:

- Quality narration and appropriate dictionary functions (text-embedded definition assistance) can both be considered positive for digital read-aloud.

- Content-connected animations can add to participants' comprehension of the story and add to positive reader experience.

- Participants may not feel the need to turn paper pages or engage in reading in the same way as their predigital facilitators (Roslund 2012).

Some transmedia materials come with multiple functions like animation, highlighted text, dictionaries, and narration options. A study of the effectiveness of transmedia materials functions places the functionalities into two discrete categories: considerate and inconsiderate. Functions noted as considerate serve to enhance and support the linear nature of the story, supporting the participants' comprehension and story retention. The functions deemed inconsiderate may detract from, rather than enhance, the storyline (Roslund 2012).

Animation and dictionaries are common functions in transmedia. A study of 43 transmedia materials discovered that almost one-third of the sources included distracting games that were inconsiderate and did not support the story. How do we know if functions are considerate or inconsiderate? To find out we need to question the following:

- Are they necessary to support the plot?
- Do the actions add to the story or encourage passive engagement?
- Can participants skip them altogether and still follow the story?
- Do they encourage attention to the story or passive distraction?

Dictionary functions allow participants to click on challenging words and see a definition, along with a considerate example of the word in a more descriptive sentence that references the story. In a recent study, readers using the dictionary function had higher story comprehension scores. Facilitators should place considerate dictionary functions high on the list for inclusion in their read-alouds by asking the following questions:

- Is there a dictionary function present in the transmedia?
- What are the definitions like?
- Do they use context from the story itself?
- How easy is it for readers to access the dictionary?
- Is it too complicated to locate (Roslund 2012)?

Optional quizzes are present in many transmedia material offerings and can be encouraging or discouraging factors of participant transmedia use. The transmedia quiz can be accessed at the end of a readings portion or at the end of the complete transmedia information text. The artful placement of the quiz within the multimedia text, format, and focus of quizzes can be another marker of quality:

- Does the quiz ask pertinent questions to the storyline, themes, character development, and contain visual aspects?
- Is the quiz challenging but accessible to participants who may vary in reading levels?
- Do some questions ask readers to "look beyond" the story and apply concepts to real-life situations (Roslund 2012)?

Guidelines for choosing transmedia read-aloud books across the ages should help facilitators focus on accessibility bound by interest and ability level (in both reading and technology). Differing ages possess a spectrum of capabilities informed by curiosity that can drive transmedia materials selection. The age designations chosen are infants, toddlers, preschoolers, elementary, middle, high, and lifelong learners.

Infants are stimulated by sight and sound. Choose transmedia materials with:

- Bright, colorful multimedia visuals.
- Familiar people, animals, and objects illustrated or animated.
- Rhythmic sounds and exciting words highlighted or with embedded dictionary function.
- Short, easy-to-listen-to texts with embedded audio.
- Emphasis on accessibility and usability.

Toddlers like books about things that spark their curiosity. Choose transmedia materials with:

- Rhymes and silly nonsense words or phrases as embedded audio.
- Phrases that are repeated predictably embedded audio.
- Engaging multimedia visuals.
- Familiar themes highlighted or with embedded dictionary function.
- Emphasis on accessibility and usability.

Preschoolers are an ideal audience for digital read-aloud activities. Many preschoolers who are pre-readers even enjoy hearing longer materials read to them. Choose transmedia materials:

- That have diverse subjects highlighted or with embedded dictionary function.
- In poetry and nonfiction formats with multimedia visuals.
- With rich language, meaningful plots, compelling characters, and engaging multimedia visuals.

Also consider the following questions when choosing transmedia materials to read aloud with preschoolers:

- Is the transmedia material of quality?
- Will the participant find the transmedia material relevant to his or her culture and life?
- Will the transmedia material spark conversation?
- Will the transmedia material inspire the participant to engage in another transmedia material experience or a cross-curricular topic, author, genre?
- Is the transmedia material memorable?
- Will the participant want to experience the transmedia material again (NWREL)?

Also consider the following questions when choosing transmedia material to read aloud with elementary, middle, high, and lifelong-learner participants:

- Is the transmedia material of quality?
- Will the participant find the transmedia material relevant to his or her culture and life?
- Will the transmedia material spark conversation?
- Will the transmedia material inspire the participant to engage in another authentic topic, author, genre, engaging cross-curricular topic engagement?
- Is the transmedia material memorable?
- Will the participant be inspired to continue engaging and exploring (NWREL)?

Preparing to Present a Digital Read-Aloud

So if we are to venture into digital read-aloud, how should we prepare? The process of planning for a digital read-aloud is similar to planning a more traditional read-aloud, though facilitators will need to commit to an additional level of planning: the creation of a backup plan in case of technology issues.

- Set the scene well; create an environment in which digital read-aloud is enjoyable and can support digital needs.
- Complete a run-through of the selected transmedia materials ahead of time to avoid surprises.
- Creatively edit when necessary.
- Read and direct students with expression and enthusiasm.
- Select the appropriate materials to digitally support the text in a meaningful way.
- Make time to present digital read-aloud sessions.
- Make it interactive; have participants become actively involved.
- Select carefully when reading to older participants between materials that are appropriate for hearing and those that work better for individual reading.
- Handle failure with grace and have a backup plan in case of technology issues (Paganelli 2016).

Proper planning and preparation for action will help the process toward delivery. Practicing prior to implementing the digital read-aloud can help isolate and respond to issues. Table 3.2 contains *The Read Aloud Handbook*'s thoughts for selecting books to use during read-aloud with an adjusted guide

Table 3.2   Tips for Selection of Digital Transmedia Read-Aloud Adapted and Adjusted from Jim Trelease's *The Read-Aloud Handbook*

Read-Aloud Handbook Book Selection	Digital Read-Aloud Transmedia Materials Selection
Selections should include a wide variety of genre.	Selections should include a wide variety of genre and media to engage students.
Selections should be age appropriate.	Selections should be age appropriate and aligned with technology proficiency of the students.
Listening levels and reading levels are different.	Listening levels and engagement levels are different.
Select books that will engage students.	Select materials that will engage students.
Competition for participant's attention is strong.	Competition for participant's attention is strong.
Display enjoyment for the book selected.	Display enjoyment for the transmedia materials selected.
Select books that lend themselves to extending the story time with projects such as art, drama, reader's theater, or writing (Trelease 2006).	Select transmedia materials that lend themselves to extending the digital story time with cross-curricular elements (Trelease 2006).

for digital read-aloud transmedia materials selection. Note that the differences for material selection are minor and foster engagement and added media.

The selection of transmedia materials is followed by the selection of the technology delivery method. The selection of the technology delivery method is a multifaceted process that must be explored so facilitators can be confident of appropriate implementation. If the delivery technology does not match the need, it can have an adverse impact on the digital read-aloud experience. The following questions will allow a thoughtful selection process:

- What types of devices are available, supported, and match participant skill level?

- What is our budget? How will this impact delivery style?

- Digital read-aloud setup: is one-on-one, small group, large group, or personalized learning appropriate?

- Are participant needs for specific cross-curricular learning or a selected authentic topic?

Table 3.3   Tips for Preparing to Read Aloud with Digital Transmedia Adapted and Adjusted from Jim Trelease's *The Read-Aloud Handbook*

Read-Aloud Handbook Guide	Digital Transmedia Read-Aloud Guide
Create an environment in which story time and reading are enjoyable.	Create an environment in which story time and reading are enjoyable and can support digital needs.
Read the story ahead of time to avoid surprises.	Complete a run-through of the selected materials ahead of time to avoid surprises.
Creatively edit when necessary.	Creatively edit when necessary.
Read with expression and enthusiasm.	Read and direct participants with expression and enthusiasm.
Select books that lend themselves to extending the story time with projects such as art, drama, reader's theater, or writing.	Select the appropriate materials to digitally support the text in a meaningful way.
Make time to present story time sessions.	Make time to present digital story time sessions.
Have participants become actively involved in the story time.	Have participants become actively involved in the digital story time.
Select carefully when reading to older students between books that are appropriate for hearing and those for individual reading (Trelease 2006).	Select carefully when reading to older students between materials that are appropriate for hearing and those for individual reading.
	Have a backup plan in case of technology issues (Trelease 2006).

In the planning process, focus on active engagement, not passive through cross-curricular digital read-aloud. Search for ways to engage the participants that encourage brains-on, hands-on, and critical thinking. Participants work well in a challenging multimedia, multimodal environment that represents the cross-curricular digital read-aloud wild west. Tips for preparing to read-aloud with digital transmedia can be found in Table 3.3.

Planning for Cross-Curricular Digital Read-Aloud

Planning for cross-curricular read-aloud requires deliberate forethought and methodology. The methodology for cross-curricular implementation listed below outlines steps that encourage meaningful deliberation toward an ultimate goal of creating a digital read-aloud experience that meets the needs of the participant audience.

- Select a theme. When selecting a theme, it is important to engage meaningfully: a real-world, authentic topic will help participants connect with the read-aloud.

- Choose a guiding question. The goal is to select a guiding question that is the focus for all the transmedia information that naturally emerges. Identify cross-curricular questions that can be asked about the authentic topics that have been selected. Identify transmedia technology for incorporation. Within cross-curricular instruction, transmedia technology becomes the means for developing interest and engagement. Selecting authentic topics and standards from the subject areas to be integrated can be useful. The transmedia materials for the authentic topics are varied in terms of interest, genre, origin, and level of difficulty (Harb 2007; Vogt 1997). Narrative literature-style transmedia material anchors the authentic topic.

- Identify a range of appropriate multimodal resources. During selection of cross-curricular materials, the concept of supportive transmedia materials should be addressed. Call on experts in some cases to help explore authentic topics and selective embracing of transmedia materials that meet the need for multimodality, including Web 2.0 tools, websites, eBooks, traditional books, magazines, brochures, maps, and any other as deemed necessary.

Developing a Schedule for Cross-Curricular Digital Read-Aloud

Developing a cross-curricular read-aloud schedule requires selecting a time frame appropriate for the level of participant technology and activity engagement. Planning a schedule for cross-curricular digital read-aloud is important. Some prefer immersion in which all transmedia information revolves around the theme, subject, or format. Whatever the facilitator's choice, it is important to keep in mind participants' interests and attention spans, as well as the availability of transmedia materials and technology. When facilitating a cross-curricular read-aloud for the first time, it helps to gauge participant interest and involvement and to be ready to modify the schedule as needed. Due to the flexible nature of cross-curricular read-aloud, flexibility and change are possible.

Activities may be directed by the facilitator or by the participants themselves. When the facilitator is scheduling or introducing a new authentic topic, they should generate enthusiasm for the cross-curricular topic while assessing, activating, and building background knowledge about the concept. Transmedia material and associated activities should stimulate engagement on multiple levels. Once the theme is launched, participants begin to engage in the read-aloud, discussing and researching, creating and generating. The facilitator monitors the schedule.

The schedule will depend in part on the type of cross-curricular implementation of the digital read-aloud chosen. The following are five ways that cross-curriculum digital read-alouds can be designed: parallel integration, infusion integration, infusion curriculum integration, multidisciplinary integration, and transdisciplinary integration. A description of each cross-curricular approach is listed below.

- Parallel integration is when two facilitators with differing specialty areas focus on a theme in a cross-curricular fashion.

- Infusion integration is a digital read-aloud focusing on multiple subject areas on the same theme with varying transmedia technology–driven activities.

- Infusion curriculum integration: this type of integration occurs when a facilitator "infuses" other subjects into the digital read-aloud.

- Multidisciplinary curriculum integration requires two or more facilitators of different specialty areas who agree to address the same theme with a common digital read-aloud activity.

- Transdisciplinary curriculum integration is the most integrated of all types of cross-curricular digital read-aloud. It also requires the most planning and cooperation between facilitators.

In these scenarios, two or more subjects share authentic topics that facilitators deliver to the participants with accompanying transmedia technology integration within the digital read-aloud.

Conclusion

Planning for the digital read-aloud can be a formidable task. Challenging decision-making capacity based on thoughtfulness focused on participants' demographics, needs, interests, and desires, together with the use of cross-curricular methods and with selected transmedia materials and grouping, can create a well-organized experience. Careful planning in these areas creates the opportunity to focus on the selection of transmedia materials. Information for the digital read-aloud can begin in the categories of augmented reality, dynamic dialogue, story author, and code author that will inspire and engage participants.

CHAPTER FOUR

Implementation of the Digital Read-Aloud

We are almost ready to implement the digital read-aloud; it can be an exhilarating, daunting, and foreign-feeling task during your first experience.

Allison Tran stated in a blog post that "The first time I saw digital read-aloud in action, I was amazed to see how effectively we can engage an audience with a book app. . . . Watching an expert share a book app was like a lightbulb going off in my head, and the first time I actually got to try it myself was most definitely another lightbulb experience. But I'm not going to lie: it was also AWKWARD" (Tran 2014). Satisfaction with the initial implementation of digital read-aloud can be greatly improved through a growth mind-set; we must understand that adding technology to the familiar read-aloud can and likely will have challenges. Through proper planning, technology management, and participant management, challenges in the digital read-aloud environment can be addressed.

Manage the Technology in Your Environment during the Digital Read-Aloud

Manage the technology in your environment during the digital read-aloud with forethought and care. Technology management can be a formidable challenge: "Despite the fact that I've done read-aloud with print books for seven years, despite the fact that I'm comfortable in front of a crowd, despite the fact that I'm a regular iPad user—wow, attempting to manipulate the iPad while referring to the screen while interacting with the audience was more challenging than I expected" (Tran 2014).

What available technologies can be used? We have a multitude of options, and each has its own opportunities and challenges. It's necessary to select a multiscreen delivery system that will be the appropriate method to display the selected transmedia materials and enable both the content topic and digital read-aloud participants. Here are some possible technologies:

- Computers
- Cell phones
- iPods/iPads
- Televisions
- DVD/CD
- Websites
- Web 2.0 tools
- Printers
- Cameras
- 3D printers
- Robots
- Breakout boxes

The aforementioned technologies for digital read-aloud delivery enable creativity, but they're not without implementation challenges. Being prepared for a read-aloud is important. Being prepared when doing a digital read-aloud is critical for management of participant experience. If the technology takes time to prepare before beginning the read-aloud, it can stall momentum and allow participant engagement to drop. When engagement is impacted, it can lead to in-group talking and off-task technology behaviors. The following tips can help keep technology functioning when and how desired to encourage engagement and on-task behavior during the digital read-aloud.

- Being able to view participant computer screens will help to ensure engagement with the digital read-aloud. Placement of technology, seating, presentation podium, and transition areas are critical to success.

- It is also important to consider the ownership of the screen delivery technology and how long it can be employed. If the screen delivery technology is on loan or shared with others, proper technology scheduling for the digital read-aloud can become of paramount importance.

- Movement and proximity support of the digital read-aloud facilitator will help to ensure engagement. If you circulate around to all participants, they will have an increased level of commitment to the experience, as you have shown a commitment to their involvement.

- When using websites it is important to create ease of access at all age levels to ensure the ability to participate in an effective and positive manner. This can be accomplished through bookmarking, quick response codes (QR codes), and hyperlinking. These technology tools create one degree of separation between the participant and the experience. Participants will not need to type in long URL chains or click on multiple links, which allows focus on time saving and usability.
- If screen delivery technology issues occur, such as remotes or clickers that don't work, it can derail the read-aloud experience altogether, so it is good to have a backup plan in place.

The digital read-aloud environment could benefit from an acceptable use policy (AUP). The AUP can be used to establish clear rules and procedures for participants' use of screen delivery technology in the digital read-aloud that can be included in the acceptable use policy.

The sections of the AUP could include but aren't limited to the following:

- Introduction and importance.
- Responsibilities of participants.
- Expectations of participants.
- Unacceptable use of the Internet.
- Guidelines for personal safety.
- Responses to violations.
- How to ask for help (Bishop and Cahall 2012).
- Does your environment need a sign-out and sign-in policy? If so, make it clear and accessible.
- Make sure to address the "bring your own device" (BYOD) use of technology in the digital read-aloud environment.

The sections will differ based on the needs of the participant and facilitator. The needs can be impacted by activity, age, and expectation. Diversity of requirement has created a boundless supply of diverse AUP available for public viewing as close as your browser. Search for the environment, age level, and type of technology usage to assemble your own customized AUP (being sure to cite your sources).

The environment can be made more inviting by the facilitator greeting and attitude. Those who feel welcomed will take more ownership and care with the environment. The design of the environment can be an enabling or disabling factor for movement, management, and engagement effectiveness. It is also important to consider all participants in the environment. The design of the environment can set the stage for a successfully planned digital read-aloud.

Ask yourself the following questions prior to implementation to gain a greater understanding of your environment and how digital technology inclusion will work in your space.

- Is the supportive technology located in my area or am I borrowing? How could this impact delivery?
- Where is my technology located in the environment? How could this impact delivery?
- Does this location work for the digital read-aloud? Would a reorganization impact delivery?
- Will the participant positioning allow for proper participation in the digital read-aloud? Would a reorganization impact delivery?

The following tips can help create a digital read-aloud environment ready for participant use of technology. Technology-related issues can be frustrating if they impact digital read-aloud delivery. Here are some things to consider as factors in the environment that can be changed to help give a more positive participant and facilitator experience with digital read-aloud.

- Use precorrection to outline possible challenges related to technology use in the environment, such as key words for transition related to technology to help ensure the participants are able to move through the transmedia material effectively.
- Use attention-getting methods such as hand clapping, finger snapping, or verbal cues to ensure all instructions are being heard to help with time management.
- Place all browser windows on needed pages and pull-up apps needed for the digital read-aloud.
- Feel free to redirect usage as needed.
- Vary your transmedia format use in the digital read-aloud (Davis 2015).
- Always have a Plan B: without a plan to transition from a digital read-aloud component to an analog experience, you are planning to fail.
- Keep the technology integration simple, and match ability of facilitator and participant (Marcinek 2014).
- Orienting participants away from distractions whenever possible can set them up for the best opportunity for success.

Sometimes the technology use in digital read-aloud can be augmented in small ways to make a big difference. The following implementation ideas make for a more smoothly implemented digital read-aloud.

- Always run through the technology to be used in the digital read-aloud *before* presenting it to the participants.

- Type directions for frequently used computer operations.
- Have participants turn *off* their monitors when you're giving directions.
- Print out step-by-step instructions.
- Post technology-related instructions and rules (Starr 2013).

Managing the Participants during the Digital Read-Aloud

Read-aloud management can be challenging. Adding on the technology component to create the digital read-aloud experience can add another level of complication. Following the guidelines below can ease the transition to a more technology-rich digital read-aloud environment.

- Establish and implement acceptable use policy early and revisit as needed.
- Use consistent techno-vocabulary when giving commands; this will help participants understand and give them the power to implement commands without frequent repeats.
- During digital read-aloud, facilitate like a shark; constant movement around participants in the learning environment can equal constant engagement.
- Address off-task-with-technology moments early and with precorrection.
- When participants are doing hands-on engagement, encourage uniform device position. This will allow a quick visual check of participant on-task behavior.
- Think outside the book, and feel free to use multiple types of screen delivery system technologies with differing levels of hands-on student engagement (Davis 2015).

Managing participants with technology in the digital read-aloud should be in part influenced by age.

Pre-K participants can display brutal honesty; meet that with precorrection and positive reinforcement of desired behaviors. Children are easily distracted at this age, so it is best to use a relatively short read. Use attention-getting techniques that are appropriate for the area setup. Are the participants seated on the floor, at a desk, standing, or with a screen delivery system for the transmedia? A positive example is the "Give Me Five" technique that consists of asking children to have "eyes on speaker, mouths closed, hands raised, ears listening, and brain thinking"—these are all accompanied by body motions to help focus the attention. This can be done in many ways with visual, verbal, and physical techniques. Don't be afraid to arrange participant grouping seating to support best engagement.

Set expectations for the type of distinct environment being used. Clear instructions are key. If seated on the floor, Pre-K participants should listen carefully, keep hands and feet to themselves, be kind to others, and respect others and their things. Seating children at a desk could be problematic and should be primarily related to short tasks and take into account the challenges of transition. Seating them at a computer table could also be problematic.

If activities are involved, effective movement of participants can be accomplished with several techniques. You can allow students to move to stations or leave based on grouping or on type of clothing, birthday, names, eye color, or any other positive identifier.

Elementary-aged participants can easily understand and follow rules set for the digital read-aloud experience. This age group can stay on task for 20- to 30-minute segments, which can open up the read-aloud experience to longer reads. This age group likes to learn by doing, so activities can be particularly motivating.

- Greeting each individual can be positive.
- Use a calm and positive demeanor.
- Instruct participants to ask critical questions and raise your hand first.
- Use creative response methods for questioning.

Set expectations for the type of environment being used. Clear instructions are key to a successful participant experience. If participants are seated on the floor, they should listen carefully, keep hands and feet to themselves, be kind to others, and respect others and their things. If participants are seated at a desk, they should engage in primarily short tasks that involve minimal transition. Participants seated at a computer table should primarily engage in short tasks that involve little transition. Allowing participants to make choices and have a voice in decision making can add to positive behavior.

Effective movement of participants when activities are involved can be accomplished with several techniques. Allow students to move to stations or leave based on grouping or on questions related to topics of popular interest, favorite activities, or would-you-rather answers.

Middle-school-aged participants as a group are desirous of acceptance and inclusion from peers and can be ready for the read-aloud experience to address personal and social issues. This age group can stay on task for 30 or more minutes, which can open up the digital read-aloud experiences to chapters from longer transmedia reads. This age group enjoys rules but also tests the limits of situational authority.

- Greeting each individual can be positive.
- Confidence and consistency are key.
- Not embarrassing them is of paramount importance.
- Building relationships is important.

Asking questions that relate to students' personal life experience will help to foster a relaxed atmosphere of inclusion. The participant engagement should be led by positive direction, correction, and creative response methods for questioning, allowing for positive participant experience.

Set expectations for the type of environment being used. Fairness and consistency are key. Seating participants on the floor should be avoided, unless you have a large area or are outside. Sitting at a desk or at a computer table is optimal as it respects boundaries and allows for greater screen-delivery-system control for the more complex tasks that can be addressed with middle-school-aged participants.

Effective movement of middle-school-aged participants when activities are involved can be accomplished with several techniques. Use attention getters that require little sound such as single tones or silent single hands being raised. Using signals can be positive. If the attention getters allow for a moment to gain students' attention, that can allow for participant conversations to be concluded and attention to be gained without the need for repetition or request.

Our high-school-aged participants may at first appear to be adults but are still developing in their progress toward adulthood. This age group is both internally and externally motivated. They are experimenting with adult relationships. High-school-aged participants strive to understand the relevance of activities and look for supportive adults. They hunger for agency and want to establish goals and lifelong strategies for success. Providing self-expression opportunities is optimal.

It is important to set high group expectations and define your role as facilitator. Find connections with topics that impact high-school-aged participants. Explore areas of common care. Positive humor is welcomed, but sarcasm toward individual participants can have a negative impact. It is important to be friendly and greet all who enter the read-aloud environment. Make sure participants are grouped with comfort of engagement in mind. Once the environment rules are set, high-school-aged participants can provide positive behavior through peer pressure (Bishop and Cahall 2012).

Lifelong learner management may include increased facilitator support with accessing and manipulating technology, if participants are unfamiliar with it. State the environmental rules prior to digital read-aloud inclusion. Mixed-aged groupings are possible in the digital read-aloud space. Being aware of the strategies related to each of the groups and then implementing them, as needed, can be positive.

The aforementioned age-grouping strategies for the digital read-aloud will work quite well with the following diverse populations. In 2020 it is projected that one in two school-aged participants will be considered a minority. This minority could be reflective of race, culture, religion, sexual orientation, or gender identity. School-aged children with special needs are on the rise. Some participants in the read-aloud who may require support for a shared experience are those with the following:

- Mental disabilities
- Learning disabilities
- Emotional disabilities
- Physical disabilities (visual, auditory, and mobility)
- Chronic illnesses
- Attention deficit disorders
- At-risk backgrounds
- Transient family backgrounds (migrant and/or homeless) (Bishop and Cahall 2012)

The most salient strategy can be simple awareness. Having knowledge of the learner will safeguard the digital read-aloud experience from unintentionally insulting the participant. Deliberate effort and planning will help reach each group and each participant where they are and ensure that all come to the read-aloud with the same equitable opportunity to experience a feeling of acceptance in a learning environment. Bishop and Cahall (2012) has outlined these general guidelines:

- Autism is a spectrum disorder that encompasses a wide range of behaviors including:
    - Learners who are on a spectrum from nonverbal to talkative.
    - Visual learners.
    - Learners who are particularly task oriented.
    - Learners who prefer the use of concrete language.
    - Those who have difficulty making and maintaining eye contact.
    - Autistic individuals may not be able to ascertain the reasons behind the actions of others.
- English-language learners (ELLs). To assist these learners,
    - Speak slowly and clearly.
    - For older ELLs, provide a listing of read-aloud–related terms and information.
    - Translated copies of transmedia are desirable if available.
- For hearing-impaired learners, learn signs to aid with the read-aloud delivery.

If the read-aloud experience is kept broad enough and respects the ideas of universal design for learning (UDL), no additional augmentations are typically needed (Bishop and Cahall 2012). UDL is the practice of providing the what, how, and why of an experience with a focus on accessibility and usability of the experience for all participants, encouraging multiple means of representation, expression, and engagement. UDL and digital read-aloud form a partnership that will explore relations between cross-curricular development and implementation. As a framework for guiding digital read-aloud, UDL provides flexibility in information presentation and student responses, reduces barriers in instruction, and provides appropriate accommodations and supports for all participants, including those with disabilities and those with limited English proficiency. The UDL is not one-size-fits-all but rather a flexible approach that can be customized and adjusted for individual needs and equity for personalized learning in the digital read-aloud (Bishop and Cahall 2012). The UDL can be a facilitator's best tool in crafting an effective and engaging digital read-aloud that allows for participant enjoyment and expression at their personal level. This focus on all participants may necessitate an examination of the traditional facilitator role.

Delivery of the Digital Read-Aloud

Delivery of the digital read-aloud should be filled with excitement, flexibility, and a positive attitude toward growth mind-set. We know that competition for participant attention is strong; by setting the tone we are able to encourage behaviors that support the digital read-aloud experience. The technology-rich digital read-aloud can help win needed engagement to spark interest that can lead to positive benefits such as literacy development skills, motivation to read, and future academic performance (Adams 1990; Anderson et al. 1985; Goldfield and Snow 1984; Keller 2012; Krashen 2004; Ross, McKechnie, and Rothbauer 2006; Trelease 2006). Display enjoyment for the materials selected and being implemented in the digital read-aloud. Our excitement can be contagious and lead to learning and engagement.

The facilitator role can be one that "empowers students to become critical thinkers, enthusiastic readers, skillful researchers and ethical users of information" (Robinson 2017). The digital read-aloud roles of the facilitator can be customized to fit the activity and screen delivery system technology being used.

A paradigm shift in the facilitator role during the digital read-aloud will be needed to move from traditional read-aloud to digital read-aloud. When planning the digital read-aloud time line, the facilitator's role should also be considered. At times the role is to lead in direct read-aloud; at other times you may serve as project manager, principal investigator, coach, or research guide.

- *The project manager.* We borrow the project manager metaphor from the design industry. It is usually used for large-scale projects where a team works together to attain a shared goal.

- *The principal investigator.* Think of the role of a principal investigator as the head of a research lab. Participants collaborate with one another and check in regularly to give advice and feedback.

- *The coach.* Good coaching can be hard to come by; it requires a certain economy of talk and limited praise with a lot of thought going into how to convey a lot of information with minimal interaction—that is, giving feedback without riding the players too much.

- *The research guide.* This resembles the role of a librarian. A librarian listens to a patron's needs, desires, and interests, and then helps connect the reader with the resources that might satisfy their hunger for knowledge. They provide strategies for finding the right materials and help unlock the powerful search tools that readers can use to find what they want now and in the future.

The facilitator styles to support customization along with examples are outlined in Table 4.1.

Setting the tone is to create procedures to support the read-aloud experience. When participants understand what is about to happen, they are more likely to follow and be able to engage with the comfort, joy, and enthusiasm we are trying to encourage. It is important to make the instructions small in number and repetitive so they become learned seamless elements of the process. Set the environment and the expectation for shared behavior. Precorrection is positive, as is modeling desired behavior. If we respond positively to the material, so will the participant. The presentation of the transmedia digital read-aloud experience can influence participant connection to the

Table 4.1   Examples of Facilitator Digital Read-Aloud Roles

(A) is like a **project manager** (oversees the team).	Watches the participants and their progress but doesn't direct discussion to the task.
(B) is like a **coach** (demonstrates economy of talk and limited praise).	"It's OK I can help you and will show you resources." "How about you use this . . . ?"
(C) is like a **principal investigator** (checks in participants regularly to provide advice and feedback).	"Why not try to make them all different?" "You want to see through something." Scaffold: the participants to find the height of the wall. "Where is your line of sight?"
(D) is like a **research guide** (helps connect the maker with needed resources).	Gave the digital read-aloud plan, instructions, and relevant apps.

material. The environment created for the digital read-aloud should draw from elements such as culture and community, cross-curricular interest, discourse, behavior, and beliefs. The digital read-aloud can be considered a social event with its own set of norms and values decided by the participants and influenced by the facilitator. "Reading aloud together creates a shared experience . . . the basis for community" (Friedman 1997).

Read-aloud can provide a scaffolding effect that can serve to raise participant knowledge and reading skills. How participants are grouped and where they sit can have a strong impact on experience. One-to-one and small groups foster involvement in the reading. Participants pay closer attention in small groups and have a greater level of response. The intimacy of the experience creates the space for that engagement. Larger groups allow for guided participation, which can lead to greater personalization of the experience, allowing for the participant to have time for consideration and an individualized response. In this way participants are allowed to rehearse understanding before sharing. To maximize delivery impact, it would be positive to consider the following recommendations:

- Situate the digital read-aloud in the desired cross-curricular context.
- Use quality transmedia information.
- Share related media of differing transmedia formats.
- Encourage personal response and cross-curricular connection building.
- Deliberate decisions about group size to encourage desired response.
- Offer variety and voice in activities allowing for participant agency.
- Reread as needed or desired (Friedman 1997).

Consider facilitator stance as an important aspect of the experience. Negative speech and bullying behavior are not tolerated in the digital read-aloud environment; this can be anticipated and controlled by participant knowledge and use of precorrective information about the topics or ideas to be explored. The most effective stance is one that focuses on the creation of positive group behavior toward participants and respect for the topics being explored. When the proper stance is executed, it can positively impact the participant experience. A stance that focuses on knowledge and respect of participants' experience and beliefs is always best. If the participants' interaction with the transmedia information has not been fully considered, unintentional results may occur that result in a negative experience.

Response to literature is a social practice that for many predates memory and harkens back to sitting in a parent's lap. The responses that emerge from literature are then wound into the culture and negotiated through nonverbal and physical cues that may be imperceptible but are nonetheless present. These cues build a shared understanding of the transmedia information. This experience can mimic that of online thumbs-up and thumbs-down. The read-aloud dance of communication can be orchestrated by the facilitator through the use of dramatic pause, emphasis, questioning, clarifying, giving feedback, support, and characterization. The nonquestioning questioner's use of declarative statements can be used to coax out comments and questions from participants. Physical proximity and eye contact can also encourage participation (Friedman 1997).

Conclusion

The digital read-aloud implementation process focuses on management of the technology, participant, and delivery. But the discussion of the digital read-aloud is a process, rather than a product, where we derive and create meaning from a shared event. Discussion is the crowdsourcing of digital read-aloud. The facilitator can encourage discussion through group and seating arrangement. Read-aloud discussion can free the participants from the facilitator and allow for agency within the read-aloud environment. Participant agency should be encouraged by having great respect for the process toward implementation, sharing reflective comments, and attempting to make connections to the greater world.

CHAPTER FIVE

Reflection on the Digital Read-Aloud

So, what did we learn from the first attempt at digital read-aloud? Did I remember to smile?

It can be easy to get caught up in concern for all of the moving parts of the digital read-aloud experience and forget to emote and engage with our participants. Participant engagement can be captured through the immersive technology-rich experiences of digital read-aloud. Once participants are engaged and digital read-aloud is implemented, the challenge then becomes how to gage success and achieve continual improvement in the digital read-aloud experience.

Learning to use digital transmedia in read-aloud is a process, one that takes practice and thoughtful, deliberate preparation. "The actual experience was exhilarating, slightly disorienting, and fun. There were moments where I felt like, Oh! Okay, I've got this! and other moments where I felt like, What am I doing up here? Where should I swipe? Where should I look?" There's a lot to think about: managing the screen delivery device, referencing the screen, interacting with the audience. "More than anything, I felt like this skill could only get better with practice, so I kind of wanted to try again immediately after finishing the story" (Tran 2014).

After attempting digital read-aloud with transmedia technology, it may be helpful to ask yourself some beginning reflective questions such as, do you use eBooks or apps in your digital read-alouds? How did you feel the first time you tried it? What helped you build confidence (Tran 2014)? It is important to informally assess participants' understanding. The following are general areas of inquiry:

- Examine the digital read-aloud experience and methods of improvement for participants.
- Examine the digital read-aloud experience and methods of improvement of delivery.
- Keep the digital read-aloud technology experience relevant through continual evaluation.

Examine the Digital Read-Aloud Experience and Methods of Improvement for Participants

To investigate areas of improvement, it's important to allow participants to share their experience with the read-aloud in an anonymous way that allows for truthful expression. When attempting to obtain this feedback, it would be positive to do an interest inquiry, monitor group needs, and facilitate multiple means of feedback. This feedback could be verbal (asking questions, story circles, or student-led questioning), physical formative (thumbs-up, thumbs-down, think-pair-share, or clicker responses), or a more formal assessment format (such as Poll Everywhere, Moodle, or Quizlet).

Examine the Digital Read-Aloud Experience and Methods of Improvement of Delivery

Evaluating delivery can be an ongoing and continuous process. Delivery involves the modeling of the appropriate use of the screen time delivery method in a technology-rich learning environment designed to support the digital read-aloud participants and facilitator. The following questions help to examine the delivery experience:

- What aspects of your digital read-aloud were implemented differently than you planned? Why did that happen?
- If you were going to implement this digital read-aloud again, what would you do differently? Why?
- What would you do the same? Why?
- What surprised you in the implementation of the digital read-aloud?
- Describe an instance or particular moment that comes to mind. Why did you pick that moment?
- What do you do well?
- What would you like to work on?
- What makes a positive experience for your participants?
- What else could you include?

Keep the Digital Read-Aloud Technology Experience Relevant through Continual Evaluation

The following digital read-aloud rubric, based on a rubric created by Dr. Jan Lewis (2000), examines enabling and disabling aspects of the implementation to determine successful areas of full implementation, partial implementation, and growth opportunities within the continuous improvement process. As you first attempt the digital read-aloud with participants, you will find this rubric helpful in your evaluation process to ensure reflective implementation of the digital read-aloud experience.

Choosing Transmedia Materials

Full implementation indicators

- The transmedia material is appropriate for this age level—they can handle the information, the emotional content, and the time frame it will take to read it.
- The transmedia material is interesting and well written.
- The transmedia material is intriguing and holds participants' attention.

Partial implementation indicators

- It works for the age group—but could be a better fit as an interest, or it's too much to deal with emotionally. Time frame not quite right—didn't hold all participants' attention because too long/too short.
- The transmedia material is mediocre. Pretty plain text, not that interesting, nothing to particularly catch participants' attention.

Growth opportunity implementation indicators

- Not a good choice of transmedia material: doesn't hold the participant's attention for any variety of reasons—quality, interest, or level.

Participant Management in the Environment

Full implementation indicators

- Participants are situated so they can see/hear. Participants can see the pictures, or some accommodation has been made so they can see.
- Participants are comfortable.
- Participants are situated so the facilitator can deal with management as they are reading.

Partial implementation indicators

- A few participants have trouble seeing/hearing.
- A few participants are not in a comfortable setting.
- A few participants are situated so that management for the facilitator is problematic.

Growth opportunity implementation indicators

- The seating situation does not allow for the majority of the participants to see/hear.
- The participants are not comfortable.
- The seating situation does not allow for good management techniques by the facilitator.

Introducing the Transmedia Materials

Full implementation indicators

- Introduce by reading the title and author. Discuss transmedia format for engagement.
- Predictions about content based on the cover appearance and title before beginning to read text.

Partial implementation indicators

- Introduce by reading the title and author. No discussion of transmedia format for engagement.
- Predictions about content based on the cover appearance and title before beginning to read text not fully implemented.

Growth opportunity implementation indicators

- No introduction by reading the title and author. No discussion of transmedia format for engagement.
- Predictions about content based on the cover appearance and title before beginning to read transmedia material not included.

Implementing the Transmedia Materials

Full implementation indicators

- Makes eye contact throughout the digital read-aloud experience.

- Uses management techniques when necessary to invite participant involvement.
- Exhibits appropriate excitement for the transmedia material.
- Acknowledges the flow of the transmedia material in deciding when to stop and ask questions or elicit discussion.
- Allows for appropriate interaction from the participants.

Partial implementation indicators

- Sometimes makes eye contact throughout the experience of the transmedia materials.
- Uses some management techniques.
- Sometimes excitement for the transmedia material is exhibited.
- Sometimes acknowledges the flow of the transmedia materials.
- Sometimes allows for appropriate interaction from the participants.

Growth opportunity implementation indicators

- Never makes eye contact throughout the transmedia material implementation.
- Management techniques are not apparent.
- Excitement for the transmedia material not exhibited.
- No acknowledgment of the flow of the transmedia material.
- Participants are not allowed to respond to the story or are allowed to take over the discussion.

Conclusion of the Transmedia Digital Read-Aloud Experience

Full implementation indicators

- Transmedia materials are brought to a closure by relating back to topic or idea.
- Many participants are interested in the transmedia materials.
- Facilitator asks appropriate guiding questions.
- Extension activities, if used, are appropriate.

Partial implementation indicators

- Transmedia materials are brought to some closure but veers from the original topic or idea.
- Some participants are interested in the transmedia material.

- Some guiding questions are not topic appropriate.
- Some extension activities do not engage participants.

Growth opportunity indicators

- No discussion to bring to closure. Or, there is little or no relationship to original topic or idea.
- Participants are not interested in the transmedia material.
- Guiding questions are not appropriate.
- Extension activities are not appropriate.

The rubric highlights why an advanced reader facilitator committed to research-based best practice for digital read-aloud support is so important. If screen time technology is being used inappropriately by participants, it can actually be detrimental to their progress toward reading comprehension skills. This is not the time for "lizard parenting," leaving participants on their own without advance reader guidance to navigate unfamiliar transmedia technology. We can facilitate and model the appropriate use of screen time technology during the digital read-aloud experience. Each time a participant reads transmedia content, they can be faced with almost limitless input and decisions, including images, video, and multiple hyperlinks that lead to even more information. As participants navigate a website, they must constantly answer questions and make decisions.

Our good readers on paper aren't necessarily good readers of transmedia materials. A differing set of skills is needed to navigate transmedia. The non-linear nature of some transmedia materials can create confusion while the enabling and disabling functions can leave readers confused in the progression. It is not a foregone conclusion that a strong reader of traditional books will be a strong reader of transmedia materials.

The shift we are seeing is that our participants are capable of attention but are more engaged with digital format mediums than those used in more traditional read-aloud environments. We can coordinate with participants to reduce the amount of time spent passively online and encourage engaged digital reading. Every little bit helps to build their pleasure-reading muscles (Korbey 2018).

"Students need to develop a reading routine, so I give my students daily time to read independently in my classroom," the article quoted Jarred Amoto as saying. "Once they find a book that hooks them, they're far more likely to unplug from technology and continue reading at home" (Korbey 2018). We, however, are not advocating for them to unplug completely. We would like for them to plug in to the digital media experience differently with an advanced reader facilitator as a guide toward digital reading success.

Assessment with cross-curricular instruction can foster the examination of salient topics, ideas, problems, and questions by engaging students in a variety of related activities from multiple disparate subjects (Vogt 1997). Self-assessment is important throughout the digital read-aloud cross-curricular implementation process. The participant and facilitator assess progress in a collaborative and supportive manner. Participants' self-assessments may help determine progress in participant learning. The important point is that the participants themselves, regardless of demographics, are involved in assessing what they have learned. Opportunities for formal and informal assessment of experience abound in the digital read-aloud format. Participants and facilitators can have discussions and ask and answer questions through multiple response measures.

In short, cross-curricular topical implementation provides opportunities for all parties involved to attain agency. Technology is dramatically altering texts and tools available to the digital read-aloud. The number of devices to run them has increased in number and diversity. Digital devices offer great promise as learning tools for digital read-aloud. Applications such as e-reading technology, changing font size on screen, using text-to-speech features to provide the dual input of text, or using the Internet to collaborate on learning activities may substantially improve the learning of many participants.

Although technology is no panacea for reading engagement issues, it can be part of the solution. Its tools must be embedded strategically within cross-curricular digital read-aloud programs. Transmedia technology tools for digital read-aloud can be more than vocabulary acquisition tools. They can aid in the creation of skilled readers (Biancorosa and Griffiths 2012).

Conclusion

If we model appropriate delivery and technology use during digital read-aloud, will participants follow that example? We can't be sure, but leading participants to view technology use and quality literature as hand-in-hand companions is a positive. Combining the positive aspects of the knowledge supporting traditional read-aloud with the digital read-aloud experience can bring heightened engagement to our digital natives. Does this engagement equal learning? It has potential. Deliberate material selections that require text quality with supportive technologies can help.

- Quality narration and appropriate dictionary functions (text-embedded definition assistance) could both be considered positive for digital read-aloud.

- Content-connected animations can add to student comprehension of the story and add to positive reader experience.

- Students may not feel the need to turn paper pages or engage in reading in the same way as their parents (Roslund 2012).

We are face-to-face with an evolving generation that views content as the end goal and traditional books as one avenue of reaching that goal. This evolution in thinking can be supported and expanded by the use of digital read-aloud. The expansion of digital read-aloud from passive to active through augmented reality, dynamic dialogue, story author, and code author format could lead to our students being content creators, not just consumers.

Examples of Digital Read-Aloud Experiences

Where is the love? In learning environments, our participants are rapidly losing the space for learning that supports joy and exploration.

Power up your read-alouds! You can do it by building reading excitement through technology and creating a digital read-aloud experience for your participants. In Part 2 we explore practical examples of transmedia materials in the Augmented Reality, Dynamic Dialog, Story Author, and Code Author categories. Each chapter follows the same format, an example of which is provided here:

Augmented Reality

The text box that begins each category includes the basic information for a particular set of transmedia materials:

Title:

Author:

Genre:

Format:

URL:

Cost:

Participant Materials

The participant materials will include all materials and technologies needed by the participant in order to fully participate in the digital read-aloud experience.

Facilitator Materials

The facilitator materials will include all materials and technologies needed by the participant who will be facilitating the digital read-aloud experience.

Standards Alignment

The following is our standards key:

American Association of School Libraries Learner Standards (AASL)

The American Association of School Librarians (2018) *National School Library Standards for Learners, School Librarians, and School Libraries* are designed to be collaborative and encourage advocacy and student-focused engagement. There are eight shared foundations, each with a key commitment and interlinked through the learning categories of Think, Create, Share, and Grow. The AASL Standards Framework for Learners can be found online at https://standards.aasl.org/framework.

International Society of Technology in Education (ISTE)

Participants must be prepared to thrive in a technological landscape that continually evolves. The standards empower student voice and ensure that learning is a student-driven process. The ISTE Standards Framework can be found online at http://www.iste.org/standards.

Description

The description can contain plot information, delivery method, and technology usage helpful hints.

Activities

This section will outline a possible activity to accomplish with the transmedia resource. This section can contain information on facilitator role, group size, and instructional method along with other information to support the activity.

* * *

Table II.1   Experience Guide for Part 2, Highlighting Subject Categories That Contain Examples with Examples of Digital Read-Aloud Experiences Organized by Resource Category, Group Size, Age Level, and Subject

Part 2				
Language Arts **Chapter 6**	**Math** **Chapter 7**	**Science** **Chapter 8**	**History/Social Studies** **Chapter 9**	**Visual Performing Arts** **Chapter 10**

Each chapter will contain an introduction and materials section.

- Each Chapter Introduction is comprised of content area—specific information on Participant Materials, Facilitator Materials, Standard Alignment, and Group Size.

- Each Chapter Materials entry for Pre-K, Elementary, Middle, and High is comprised of Augmented Reality and Dynamic Dialogue that consists of Title, Author, Genre, Format, URL, Cost, Participant Materials, Facilitator Materials, Standards Alignment, Description, and Activities. The Life-Long Learner section focuses on Story Author and Code Author experiences.

Pre-K Augmented Reality Dynamic Dialogue	*Pre-K* Augmented Reality Dynamic Dialogue	*Pre-K* Augmented Reality Dynamic Dialogue	*Pre-K* Augmented Reality Dynamic Dialogue	*Pre-K* Augmented Reality Dynamic Dialogue
Elementary Augmented Reality Dynamic Dialogue	*Elementary* Augmented Reality Dynamic Dialogue	*Elementary* Augmented Reality Dynamic Dialogue	*Elementary* Augmented Reality Dynamic Dialogue	*Elementary* Augmented Reality Dynamic Dialogue
Middle Augmented Reality Dynamic Dialogue	*Middle* Augmented Reality Dynamic Dialogue	*Middle* Augmented Reality Dynamic Dialogue	*Middle* Augmented Reality Dynamic Dialogue	*Middle* Augmented Reality Dynamic Dialogue
High Augmented Reality Dynamic Dialogue	*High* Augmented Reality Dynamic Dialogue	*High* Augmented Reality Dynamic Dialogue	*High* Augmented Reality Dynamic Dialogue	*High* Augmented Reality Dynamic Dialogue
Lifelong Learner Code Author Story Author	*Lifelong Learner* Code Author Story Author	*Lifelong Learner* Code Author Story Author	*Lifelong Learner* Code Author Story Author	*Lifelong Learner* Code Author Story Author

To power up and extend the experiences for lifelong learning, including the Story Author and Code Author categories, further extends the cross-curricular engagement experience. Standards connections used within the cross-curricular digital read-aloud experience will vary by content subject and age of participant.

The response activities most frequently associated with read-aloud are writing and drawing, followed by dramatization and construction (Hoffman, Roser, and Battle 1993). These are included along with joint media engagement as a type of co-viewing and sharing and viewing appvisory (the technology-enhanced version of readers' advisory). These are two ways to support our participants when we are not able to engage them directly.

"In the past, the digital divide described students with technology compared to those without. Today, the divide addresses students who receive instruction on how to do things with technology versus those learning how to make technology do things. Now that computer science is the highest paid career for college graduates, it is time to stop teaching students how to *push* the buttons and start teaching them how to *make* the buttons" (Adam and Mowers 2013).

Examples of cross-curricular digital read-aloud "can be found in STEM (science, technology, engineering, and math) learning and the more recently coined STEAM (science, technology, engineering, arts and math) learning. The organization of these subject areas under one collective effort represents a recent trend toward cross-curricular integration in education. Cross-curricular [digital read-alouds can] include both humanities (ELA, social studies, arts) and STEM subjects, [highlighting] the importance of creativity and collaboration, both skills that are increasingly necessary for modern employment" (Harb 2007).

The following chapters help educators, including librarians, find age-appropriate transmedia materials that will strengthen students' skills in the humanities and STEAM disciplines.

CHAPTER SIX

Language Arts

The language arts transmedia resources and digital read-aloud activities presented here offer examples designed to show a cross-section of the many available within this subject area and the transmedia material category. It is possible for these activities and others in this resource category to be stand-alone, read-aloud text experiences, creator experiences, or enhanced with personalized learning. These materials also have the potential to be enhanced with technology and its various applications. The applications are designed to support several books or stand alone through web delivery. The resources can be implemented one-on-one, small group, or as a large group activity.

The following is a Materials section designed to give hands-on practical application examples to support successful implementation. All of the transmedia materials highlighted in this section are categorized for Pre-K, Elementary, Middle, and High, then comprised of Augmented Reality and Dynamic Dialogue that consists of Title, Author, Genre, Format, URL, Cost, Participant Materials, Facilitator Materials, Standards Alignment, Description, and Activities. The Lifelong Learner section focuses on Story Author and Code Author experiences.

Pre-K

Augmented Reality

Title: *Goodnight Lad*
Author: Bradley Grimm
Genre: Picture Book
Format: Paperback book with digital application
URL: https://www.goodnightlad.com/app
Cost: Less than $5.00 per copy

Participant Materials

- Copy of the *Goodnight Lad* book
- iPad for use with the accompanying application

Facilitator Materials

- Copy of the *Goodnight Lad* book
- Access to the material will be through the iPad
- The iPad will be used to engage the augmented reality text and then mirrored to the smart board so that the entire group will be able to view and interact with the transmedia material.
- Items that would be used to get ready for bed—some that were included in the story and some that were not included in the story.

Standards Alignment

AASL: I
ISTE: 1

Description

Goodnight Lad is an augmented reality children's book, and each page comes to life with animations that you can interact with to really get into the book. Through the use of the iPad the images leap off the page and enter a world of augmented reality. A little boy who refuses to go to bed. He wants to play instead. His parents decide to take him around the world to tire him out.

Activities

The augmented reality text can be used to serve an entire group of participants. The use of a single resource can make this a cost-effective option for facilitators. The digital read-aloud experience will be supplemented with an array of materials in multiple formats, allowing a hands-on experience for participants. The *Good Night Lad* digital read-aloud will be supported with an array of items that the Pre-K participants might use when preparing for bed as a way to allow for the participants to make personal connections and postulate the story contents.

The *Good Night Lad* augmented reality text hands-on experience will be supported by a comprehension guide designed to have simple "yes" or "no" responses to engage the Pre-K learners in providing feedback on elements that were present in the story. Where participants get to share what was or was not a part of the story.

Dynamic Dialogue

Title: *The Going to Bed Book*
Author: Sandra Boynton
Genre: Picture Book
Format: Application
URL: http://play.google.come/store/apps/details?id=com.loudcrow.goingtobed
Cost: Under $10.00 per copy

Participant Materials

- Copy of *The Going to Bed Book*
- Copy of *The Going to Bed Book* application

Facilitator Materials

- Access through the website.
- Device used to interface will be the iPad.
- The iPad will be used to engage the augmented reality text and then mirrored to the smart board so that the entire group will be able to view and interact with the transmedia material.

Standards Alignment

AASL: I
ISTE: 1

Description

A silly trip all around to get to bed and become sleepy. The augmented reality text allows for participants to get hands-on technology use with the iPad and interact with the book to have impact on the experience but not the story. The application has a narrator that leads the participant through the story. This mitigates the potential for distraction present with the interactivity of the application.

Activities

The large group hands-on digital read-aloud experience is best guided by an advanced reader. The dynamic dialogue materials can become distracting and disable progress through the story. With guidance from an advanced reader facilitator, the Pre-K students will learn how to navigate transmedia text successfully. It allows the facilitator to have control of the resource and direct the participant experience. The large group read-aloud with dynamic dialog allows for the facilitator to guide the participant experience with questioning that can be supported by the texts feature of inquiry.

Elementary School

Augmented Reality

Title: *Sleep Sweet*
Author: Julianne DiBlase Black
Genre: Picture Book
Format: Paperback book works with an application to augment the presented text.
URL: http://spellboundar.com
Cost: Under $10.00 per copy

Participant Materials

- Copy of *Sleep Sweet*

Facilitator Materials

- Access to the application.
- Device to run the application will be the iPad.

Standards Alignment

AASL: I
ISTE: 1

Description

Rich in imagination, imagery, and color, *Sleep Sweet* makes a wonderfully gentle and calming addition to any quiet time or bedtime routine with augmented reality. Designed to gently relax and at the same time engage, this augmented reality book takes the reader through a series of animals with sound and visuals that encourages the animals to sleep sweet.

Activities

The one-to-one read-aloud experience is a wonderful way to engage the augmented reality text. It allows the participant to have control of the resource and the facilitator to be in a supportive role. The one-to-one participant experience would be immersive. The more traditional digital read-aloud approach will work well with this augmented reality transmedia material. Ideally, the experience is participant driven and is monitored by the facilitator.

Dynamic Dialogue

Title: *Show What You Know!*
Author: Sandra Boynton
Genre: Picture Book/Series
Format: Application
URL: k12.follett.com/lightbox
Cost: Subscription/Prices Vary

Participant Materials

- Copy of *Show What You Know!*
- Access to the *Show What You Know!* book series in the *Lightbox* application

Facilitator Materials

- Access through the website.
- Device used to interface will be the iPad.
- The iPad will be used to engage the Dynamic Dialogue text and then mirrored to the smart board so that the entire group will be able to view and interact with the transmedia material.

Standards Alignment

AASL: I
ISTE: 1

Description

In this Digital Dialogue series participant readers are able to explore the topics of *Create a Slide Show, Find a Research Topic, Find the Right Words, Give an*

Oral Presentation, Research Using Videos, and *Take Good Notes.* The text allows for participants to get hands-on technology use with the iPad and interact with the book to have impact on the experience but not the story. The application/platform has a litany of supportive digital materials. The books have embedded videos, audio narration, weblinks, printable PDF activities, Slideshows, embedded Google Maps, highlighted key concepts or words, and quizzes. All or none of the add-ons can be used to support the participant experience. The incorporation of an advanced reader guide mitigates the potential for distraction present with the interactivity of the application.

Activities

The large group hands-on digital read-aloud experience is best guided by an advanced reader. The dynamic dialogue materials can become distracting and disable progress through the story. With guidance from an advanced reader facilitator, the elementary school students will learn how to navigate transmedia text successfully. It allows the facilitator to have control of the resource and direct the participant experience. The large group read-aloud with dynamic dialog allows for the facilitator to guide the participant experience with questioning that can be supported by the texts feature of inquiry. The additional materials can be used to extend the experience for participants.

Middle School

Augmented Reality

Title: *The Fantastic Flying Books of Mr. Morris Lessmore*
Author: William Joyce
Genre: Picture Book
Format: Paperback book works with an application to augment the
   presented text.
URL: http://moonbotstudios.com/2013/01/the-fantasticflyings-books-of
   -mr-morris-lessmore-picture-book.html
Cost: Under $20.00 per copy

Participant Materials

- *The Fantastic Flying Books of Mr. Morris Lessmore* book and application will be shared with the facilitator and small group participants.

Facilitator Materials

- Copy of *The Fantastic Flying Books of Mr. Morris Lessmore*.
- Device used to access the application will be the iPad.

Standards Alignment

AASL: V
ISTE: 1

Description

The story is about a man's magical life among books. The augmented reality book can be used with or without the iPad application. The traditional book element has amazing illustrations. When the augmented reality elements are added through the use of the application the story becomes a part of the participants' surrounding with books flying across the room and narration to support pivotal areas of the story.

Activities

The small group read-aloud is perfect for a less immersive but still targeted experience of the augmented reality resource. It allows the facilitator to have control of the resource and direct the participant experience. The small group participant experience is communal and allows for greater discussion of the resource content. For the small group experience to be hands-on, allow each member of the group to lead the digital read-aloud through one of the augmented reality segments. To extend the experience, use the projected application view for the *Fantastic Flying Books of Mr. Morris Lessmore*. To accomplish this on a whiteboard, the facilitator will need to pair their device with an available projector.

Dynamic Dialogue

Title: *Jack and the Bean Stalk Children's Interactive Book*
Genre: Interactive application.
Format: Web-based application.
URL: http://playtalkread.scot/ideas/164-jack-and-the-beanstalk-interactive
   -book
Cost: Free

Participant Materials

- Copy of *Jack and the Bean Stalk Children's Interactive Book*

Facilitator Materials

- Access to the website via the Internet.
- Device used will be the computer; either Mac or PC is compatible.

Standards Alignment

AASL: IV
ISTE: 3

Description

Let your child be the hero of the story as they read through the classic story of Jack and the Beanstalk. Just enter their name to begin the story, take them to get some magic beans, and be sure to avoid the giant!

Activities

This website allows the student to have control of the resource and the facilitator to be in a supportive role. This is particularly important with this application as it can be customized. The one-to-one participant experience is immersive and has the ability to personalize the experience by including the student's name. This is a great opportunity for student voice. The group could name and create their avatar to guide through the transmedia material.

High School

Augmented Reality

Title: *Alice for iPad*
Author: Atomic Antelope
Format: Application
URL: http://itunes.apple.com/us/app/alice-for-the-ipad/id354537426
Cost: Under $5.00 per copy

Participant Materials

* *Alice for iPad* application

Facilitator Materials

* Access to the website via the Internet.
* iPad.
* Method used to project will be to share the iPad image with the smart board.

The large group read-aloud with augmented reality allows for the facilitator to guide the participant experience. It requires a single copy of the augmented reality text to be used to serve an entire group of participants.

Standards Alignment

AASL: V
ISTE: 1

Description:

Digital reimaging of the classic Lewis Carroll book engages a new generation of readers by creating an augmented reality version. The classic will come to life and reach a new generation where they live, in the digital world.

Activities

The one-to-one read-aloud experience is a wonderful way to engage the augmented reality text. It allows the student to have control of the resource and the facilitator to be in a supportive role. The one-to-one participant experience would be immersive.

The small group read-aloud is perfect for a less immersive but still targeted experience of the augmented reality resource. It allows the facilitator to have control of the resource and direct the participant experience. It will allow for greater discussion of the content materials.

Dynamic Dialogue

Title: *Inanimate Alice*
Author: Kate Pullinger and Chris Joseph
Genre: Fiction
Format: Transmedia
URL: www.inanimatealice.com
Cost: Free

Participant Materials

- *Inanimate Alice* application for each participant

Facilitator Materials

- Access will be achieved via the Internet.
- Device used will be a laptop computer.

Standards Alignment

AASL: I

ISTE: 1

Description

In the first episode, Alice is an eight-year-old game designer living in far north China. Her dad goes missing on a trip to search for oil. Alice and her mom go searching for her dad. This multiepisode story is delivered exclusively online and engages using a variety of visual and sound methods of storytelling.

Activities

The use of all three methods would highlight the text and create an opportunity of multiple means of engagement. As an introduction try using the large group read-aloud with the facilitator to guide the participant experience. It requires a single copy of the augmented reality text to be used to serve an entire group of participants. Transitioning to the one-to-one read-aloud experience method allows the participants to have control of the resource and the facilitator to be in a supportive role. Culminating in the small group digital read-aloud will support the individual needs of each participant member of the group. It will allow for a deeper and more intimate discussion of the story elements as a concluding activity.

Lifelong Learner

Story Author

Title: *Storybird*

Format: Website

Description: Participants can become authors by creating their own stories, adding text to existing professional artwork.

URL: Storybird.com

Cost: Free educator version

Standards Alignment

AASL: VI

ISTE: 6

Activity

Digital Storytelling with Storybird

eBooks and Digital Storytelling takes the ancient art of oral storytelling and engages a palette of technical tools to weave tales using images, graphics, music, and sound mixed together with the author's own story voice. We will facilitate the ultimate expression of creativity. The creation of an original piece of literature that is participant crafted and shared during the digital read-aloud experience.

<u>Resources/Materials Needed:</u>

- Computer
- Curriculum documents
- Storybird.com

<u>Your Task:</u>

You will create a digital story with at least 10 slides on your authentic topic. Be sure to review your written content before you create your project and again before you submit your project.

1. Determine how you are going to access the *Storybird* application.

2. Decide on the story you want to tell.

3. Write your story script.

4. Create a storyboard.

5. Create your digital story with the following elements:

    a. Include at least 10 slides. You may need more than 10 slides to make a complete story.

    b. Create a title screen at the beginning of your digital story.

    c. Edit your digital story if needed.

6. Share the finished product in a participant-led digital read-aloud. When completed reflect on your process and how it works to have a participant presenter.

    a. How did the *Storybird* application work for the digital story creation?

    b. What technical problems did you encounter when creating this project?

    c. How did you use this eBook/digital storytelling in your lesson plan?

    d. How did you customize the eBook/digital storytelling to your target student?

    e. How did the eBook/digital storytelling address the whole group's needs?

Code Author

Title: Novel Coding

Format: Scratch

Description: *Scratch* is a website that allows for the creation and animation of stories using drag and drop coding. The coding tiles can be arranged to control the movements and actions or the animated characters. The costumes can be augmented to allow for greater visual control and expression of the story. The sound can be adjusted to further express the story. It can allow the coded animation to share the participants' original literature creations.

URL: www.scratch.mit.edu

Cost: Free.

Standards Alignment

AASL: IV

ISTE: 6

Activity

Novel Coding

Use *Scratch* to express original literature in the form of a coded animation. We will facilitate student agency, and the facilitator role will be that of a project manager. The facilitator/project manager will only engage as needed to redirect allowing students to be self-directed and use their participant agency. The facilitator will also be aiding with technology support. It would be positive to identify possible technology-savvy participants to act as helpers when multiple participants have questions or concerns with their progress in *Scratch*.

<u>Resources/Materials Needed:</u>

- Computer

  www.scratch.mit.edu

<u>Your Task:</u>

1. Through exploration of the *Scratch* application:
   a. Recognize the three aspects of the *Scratch* application: code, costumes, and sounds. Experiment with each until you have a basic understanding. This project can be accomplished individually or in small groups.
   b. Create a scene from a novel you would like to write.
   c. Understand that the story does not need to be complete. The participants will be sharing one scene from a novel they would like to write. Encourage them to select a novel, book, or story they have read and bring life to their favorite scene.

Student Activities

Participants will:
- Load and open *Scratch*.
- Use present functionalities of code, costumes, and sound to set the stage for the novel scene.
- Participants should focus on the character selection and giving movement to the scene in the code section of *Scratch*.
- Participants should focus on the costume selection and giving visuals to the scene in the costume section of *Scratch*.
- Participants should focus on the sound selection and giving audio to the scene in the sound section of *Scratch*.
- Each participant should then create their own story scene from their original novel idea or their selected favorite, layering the code, costumes, and sounds.

This activity is designed for the participants to be able to express voice and have choice in their progress toward the completed product. The participants will be allowed to work individually or in small groups to complete the task. By encouraging choice of how to engage, the task participants will be able to exert control and increase comfort level with the task. Participants will be encouraged to write down the stories they have created or chosen.

Conclusion

Reading literature for pleasure makes learning painless. If you are enjoying your journey through a piece of transmedia text, you may not be aware that you just connected to prior knowledge and cemented a learned concept. The utilization of literature with content allows gradual exposure to transmedia materials. It allows participants to recognize that there are different purposes for reading, and reading can be adjusted to fit learning goals. The integration of quality transmedia literature into content areas can increase the amount of time participants spend with text and help to improve reading proficiency (Harb 2007).

CHAPTER SEVEN

Math

Mathematics curriculum can involve participants in the digital read-aloud relating and applying math ideas to real life. Math-related literature provides participants with beneficial experiences, as well as a multitude of other added intangibles associated with engagement. One function of the coupling of mathematics and literature is to make sense of the world around us. Through the use of literature, math can be placed into real-world contexts (Harb 2007).

The math resources and digital read-aloud activities listed reflect an offering of examples designed to show the many available within each category. It is possible for each of these and others in this resource category to be a stand-alone, read-aloud text experience, creator experience or enhanced with personalized learning. It also has the potential to be a technology-enhanced delivery by using the varied applications. The applications are designed to support math learning through reading and otherwise. The resources can be implemented with a single child, small group, or large group activity.

The following is a Materials section designed to give practical examples to support successful application. All of the transmedia materials highlighted in this section are categorized for Pre-K, Elementary, Middle, and High, then comprised of Augmented Reality and Dynamic Dialogue that consists of Title, Author, Genre, Format, URL, Cost, Participant Materials, Facilitator Materials, Standards Alignment, Description, and Activities. The Lifelong Learner section focuses on Story Author and Code Author experiences.

Pre-K

Augmented Reality

Title: *The Numberlys*
Author: William Joyce
Genre: Picture Book
Format: Book with application
URL: http://moonbotstudios.com/2014/10/numberlys-picture-book.html
Cost: Under $20.00 per copy

Participant Materials

- Copy of *The Numberlys*

Facilitator Materials

- Access via website.
- Device used is the iPad.
- Method mirroring the iPad to the projection screen.

Standards Alignment

AASL: I
ISTE: I

Description

Travel along with the Numberlys from black and white numbers to alphabet and colors on a twisting turning ride. In our story the Numberlys use numbers to develop language and make the transition into alphabetic communication. This textbook coupled with an augmented reality application extends to story from the page to the readers' environment.

Activities

The small group read-aloud is perfect for a less immersive but still targeted experience of the augmented reality resource. The book, iPad, and application would need to be available for the small group participants. The facilitator would lead the group from page to page within the text with additional instructions for the application. This would be punctuated with breaks to allow time for exploration.

Dynamic Dialogue

Title: *Less Than Zero*
Author: Stuart J. Murphy
Genre: Nonfiction
Format: eBook
URL: http://www.tumblemath.com
Cost: Subscription service prices vary based on usage.

Participant Materials

- Copy of *Less Than Zero*

Facilitator Materials

- Access via website platform with multiple transmedia materials.
- Device used is a computer.

Standards Alignment

AASL: I
ISTE: 3

Description

Perry the Penguin wants to buy an ice scooter, but he's not very good at saving. The author shows kids that they use math every day to share a pizza, spend their allowance, and even sort socks. The book and application can be used independently of each other. The Tumble Books digital dialogue transmedia contains audio, highlighting the text being read, and animation.

Activities

The large group facilitator led read-aloud engages participants with the tumble book *Less Than Zero* and is an excellent way to support learning to navigate dynamic dialog transmedia materials. The *Less Than Zero* dynamic dialog is perfect to allow for the facilitator to guide the participant through the material. It has few distractions in the form of games, quizzes, etc. The one-to-one device participant experience with facilitator leading would be immersive but needs guided advanced reader support for the Pre-K age group.

Elementary School

Augmented Reality

Title: *Easy Origami Greeting Cards*
Author: Christopher Harbo
Genre: Nonfiction
Format: Book with application
URL: https://www.amazon.com/Easy-Origami-Greeting-Cards-Experience
   /dp/1515735877/ref=sr_1_1
Cost: Less than $20.00 per copy

Participant Materials

- Copy of *Easy Origami Greeting Cards.*
- Origami paper.
- Device used would be the iPad.

Facilitator Materials

- Access through the application and use of the text.
- Device used would be the iPad.

Standards Alignment

AASL: V
ISTE: 6

Description

Want to create? Creation is just a few folds away! Learn how to build origami pigs, ducks, and teacups. With photo-illustrated instructions and augmented reality access to video tutorials in the free Capstone 4D app, you'll never get stuck on a step. Just grab some paper and start crafting!

Activities

The one-to-one read-aloud experience with the *Easy Origami Greeting Cards* text is a wonderful way to engage the augmented reality text in a hands-on experience. It allows the participant to have control of the resource and work at their own pace with the facilitator in a project manager role watching the participants and their progress but not directing the task, which allows participants to take control of their learning. The digital read-aloud with augmented reality allows for the facilitator to guide the participant experience. Using the research librarian facilitator role you can give the demonstration, instructions, and relevant apps and thus strongly support independent learning. Either facilitator style can be employed to meet recognized participant need.

Dynamic Dialogue

Title: *Making and Using Graphs*
Author: Sandra Boynton
Genre: Picture Book
Format: Application
URL: k12.follett.com/lightbox
Cost: Subscription/Prices Vary

Participant Materials

- Copy of *Making and Using Graphs*
- Copy of *Making and Using Graphs* application

Facilitator Materials

- Access through the website.
- Device used to interface will be the iPad.
- The iPad will be used to engage the augmented reality text and then mirrored to the smart board so that the entire group will be able to view and interact with the transmedia material.

Standards Alignment

AASL: V
ISTE: 5

Description

In this Digital Dialogue series participant readers are able to explore the topics of *Bar Graphs, Graphing Story Problems, Line Graphs, Pictographs, Pie Graphs,* and *Tally Carts.* The text allows for participants to get hands-on technology use with the iPad and interact with the book to have impact on the experience but not the story. The application/platform has a litany of supportive digital materials. The books have embedded videos, audio narration, weblinks, printable PDF activities, Slideshows, embedded Google Maps, highlighted key concepts or words, and quizzes. All or none of the add-ons can be used to support the participant experience. The incorporation of an advanced reader guide mitigates the potential for distraction present with the interactivity of the application.

Activities

The large group hands-on digital read-aloud experience is best guided by an advanced reader. The dynamic dialogue materials can become distracting and disable progress through the story. With guidance from an advanced reader facilitator, the elementary students will learn how to navigate transmedia text successfully. It allows the facilitator to have control of the resource and direct the participant experience. The large group read-aloud with dynamic dialog allows for the facilitator to guide the participant experience with questioning that can be supported by the texts feature of inquiry. As a bonus all of the materials or none of the audio, videos, activities, weblinks, slideshows, interactive maps, quizzes and key words can be used or not depending on need.

Middle School

Augmented Reality

Title: *iRobot: Battle with Bots! (iExplore)*
Author: Clive Gifford
Genre: Picture Book/Informational Text
Format: Book with application
URL: https://www.amazon.com/iRobot-Battle-iExplore-Clive-Gifford/dp
     /1783122706/ref=sr_1_17
Cost: Less than $20.00 for the book and the application is free

Participant Materials

*   Copy of *iRobot: Battle with Bots! (iExplore)*

Facilitator Materials

*   Access will be through the application.
*   Device used will be the iPad.

Standards Alignment

AASL: IV
ISTE: 5

Description

Watch robots come to life, thanks to the digital magic of augmented reality. Use the book, app, and device to build your own robot and program it to move. Fly a drone, and engage in battle! Just place your tablet or smartphone near the visual icon on the page. This will activate *iRobot* information about machines and how they work.

Activities

The one-to-one read-aloud experience will be participant led, and the participants will engage in pairs. It will allow students to see the real-world application of math concepts. Participants will be able to manipulate factors of the robot creation and then discuss how this improves the experience. Each experience can be charted on graph paper to measure the experience. To connect the engagement, it would be positive to have participants write down questions and connections with math as they view the transmedia resource remotely.

Dynamic Dialogue

Title: *Sir Conference at the Fraction Faire*
Author: Cindy Neuschwander
Genre: Picture Book
URL: http://www.tumblemath.com
Cost: Subscription service prices vary based on usage.

Participant Materials

- A copy of *Sir Conference at the Fraction Faire* application

Facilitator Materials

- Access via website platform with multiple transmedia materials.
- Device used is a computer.
- Pizza or another food to divide into equal parts.

Standards Alignment

AASL: V
ISTE: 5

Description

Sir Conference at the Fraction Faire is a math adventure. It takes readers through a faire and the experience of using fractions in fabricated real-world situations. It includes mystery, vocabulary, and adventure to encourage mathematical understanding. The book and application can be used independently of each other. The Tumble Books digital dialogue transmedia contains audio, highlighting the text being read, and animation.

Activities

Participants will be allowed to have paper and pencil and draw math representations and related art. The large group read-aloud with augmented reality allows for the facilitator to guide the participant experience. It requires a single copy of the augmented reality text to be used to serve an entire group of participants. The use of a single resource can make this a cost-effective option for facilitators; it does not require multiple access to the transmedia or multiple computers. As a culminating activity the large group will be given a pizza and will need to work out how many slices to create.

High School

Augmented Reality

Title: *Virtual and Augmented Reality for Dummies*
Author: Paul Mealy
Genre: Informational Book
Format: Audible Book
URL: https://www.amazon.com/Virtual-Augmented-Reality-Dummies
    -Computer/dp/1119481341/ref=sr_1_1
Cost: Under $20.00 per copy

Participant Materials

•   Copy of *Virtual and Augmented Reality for Dummies*

Facilitator Materials

- Access to the text and search engine for further research
- Device of computer needed for research through a browser

Standards Alignment

AASL: III
ISTE: 6

Description

The concept of augmented reality (AR) is quickly becoming a driving force in the next technological revolution. If you want to get in on the action, this book helps you understand what these technologies are, how they're being used, and how they'll affect the near future. The book gives background information designed to be at beginner level.

Activities

The digital read-aloud is perfect for a text to execute small research teams. It allows the participant to have control of the resource and direct the personalized learning experience. The small group participant experience would be communal and allow for greater discussion of the research process. The facilitator role would be as the principal investigator. As principal investigator, the facilitator would be checking in to monitor progress regularly and providing needed advice and direction. The participants will be asked to identify one of the roles of math in augmented reality.

Dynamic Dialogue

Title: *Google Hangouts/Expert Guest Read-Aloud*

Author: The author would be the expert math guest that will do a reading of their choice related to math. Ideally, it would be a math professional.

Genre: Informational

Format: Human Library, using an expert in the educational environment to stand in for a transmedia text through the use of digital communication software such as Google Hangouts.

URL: https://hangouts.google.com

Cost: Free

Participant Materials

- None needed

Facilitator Materials

- Access via computer to Google Hangouts.
- Device will be a computer.

Standards Alignment

AASL: IV
ISTE: 6

Description

The transmedia digital read-aloud will be engaging dynamic virtual dialog through invited expert guest reader.

Activities

The Google Hangouts with the expert guest as human library would take the form of an interview with a math professional. It would allow for preplanned questioning as well as more spontaneous questioning and free flowing discussion. It allows the facilitator and participant to share control of the experience. An opportunity to write out questions prior would be beneficial, along with deciding in advance which participants will ask the questions. The expert experience will allow the large group to make connections with math in a professional exploration.

Lifelong Learner

Story Author

Title: *Storyboard That Masked Math Hero*

Format: Website

Description: Participants can become authors by creating their own stories in the form of comic strips, adding text to existing professional artwork that can be dragged and dropped into the comic strip storyboard.

URL: Storyboarthat.com

Cost: Free version

Standards Alignment

AASL: VI
ISTE: 6

Activity

Storyboard That Masked Math Hero

The *Storyboard That* application allows participants to take the art of comic storytelling and engage a palette of technical tools to weave the provided images together to create their own super hero. We will facilitate the expression of creativity through the visual representation of a Math Hero—the creation of an original Math Hero that is participant crafted and shared during the digital read-aloud experience. The participants will engage with agency while they tell the story behind the Math Hero and share the comic book style visual representation.

Resources/Materials Needed:

- Computer
- Storyboardthat.com

Your Task:

You will create a Math Hero with at least five unique characteristics. Be sure your five unique characteristics have reasons rooted in the Math Hero's backstory.

1. Determine how you are going to access the *Storyboard That* application.
2. Decide on the Math Hero to create and their backstory.
3. Write your storyboard script.
4. Create a storyboard.
5. Create your digital story with the following elements:
    a. Include at least five characteristics. You may need more than five characteristics to make a complete comic story.
    b. Create a title screen at the beginning of your comic story.
    c. Edit your comic story if needed.
6. Share the finished product in a participant-led digital read-aloud. When completed reflect on your process and how it works to have a participant presenter.
    a. How did the *Storyboard That* application work for the comic story creation?
    b. What technical problems did you encounter when creating this project?

   c.   How did you use this comic storytelling in your presentation?

   d.   How did you customize the comic storytelling to your target participants?

   e.   How did the comic storytelling address the whole group's needs?

Code Author

Title: *Minecraft*

Format: Application

Description: *Minecraft* is a game about creation, survival, placing blocks, and going on adventures. It can also drive math exploration, creating your own math experience utilizing the game coding.

URL: www.minecraft.net

Cost: Varies depending on version and functions.

Standards Alignment

AASL: I

ISTE: 4

Activity

Minecraft Area and Volume

Use Minecraft to create and solve problems involving area and volume. We will facilitate student agency, and the facilitator role will be that of a project manager, engaging only as needed to redirect, allowing students to be self-directed and use their participant agency.

Resources/Materials Needed:

- Computer
- Minecraft.net

Your Task:

1. Through exploration:

   a.   Recognize volume as an attribute of three-dimensional space.

   b.   Write and interpret numerical expressions.

   c.   Understand that volume can be measured by finding the total number of same-size units of volume required to fill the space without gaps or overlaps.

Introduce the concept of area and volume. Show to participants how you can use materials available in Minecraft to fill space. Explain to participants that volume can be measured by finding the total number of same-size units of volume required to fill the space without gaps or overlaps.

Student Activities

Participants will:

- Load and open Minecraft.

- Use present materials to fill areas and record the amounts it took.

- Participants should record the answers to their work.

- Each participant should then create their own puzzles using multiple blocks within Minecraft, to create shapes.

This activity is adapted from one shared on minecraft.net. They have many lesson plans that are across the curriculum and can be cross-curricular in application. The complex exploration and problem solving would be challenging to guide in a traditional read-aloud environment. By anchoring the participant math progress, you can discuss how math problem solving can be expressed as a story. Participants will be encouraged to write down the results of their digital guided read-aloud activity experience.

Conclusion

Mathematics transmedia digital read-aloud can involve participants in relating and applying math ideas to real life. Math-related literature such as *Sir Conference at the Fraction Faire* provides participants with beneficial, describing experiences, built on concrete examples that drive engagement. The joining of mathematics and literature can bring abstract concepts to reality and help participants connect. Through the use of literature, math can be placed into real-world contexts (Harb 2007).

CHAPTER EIGHT

Science

Many have suggested that scientific learning may be enhanced through the use of quality literature. The careful examination of science concepts and the understanding that they have their own language and vocabulary can make the exploration of informational transmedia materials important learning experiences. Literature promotes the appropriate study of science with emphasis on topic and ideas that bridge multiple cross-curricular content areas (Harb 2007).

The science resources and read-aloud activities listed reflect an offering of examples to represent the many available within the category. It is possible for each of these and others in this resource category to be stand-alone, read-aloud text experiences, creator experiences, or be supplemented with personalized learning. It also, has the potential to be a technology—enhanced delivery by using the varied Web 2.0 tools. The applications are designed to support science learning through reading and otherwise. The resources can be implemented with a single child, small group, or large group activity.

The following is a Materials section designed to give hands-on practical application examples to support successful implementation. All of the transmedia materials highlighted in this section are categorized for Pre-K, Elementary, Middle, and High, then comprised of Augmented Reality and Dynamic Dialogue that consists of Title, Author, Genre, Format, URL, Cost, Participant Materials, Facilitator Materials, Standards Alignment, Description, and Activities. The Lifelong Learner section focuses on Story Author and Code Author experiences.

Pre-K

Augmented Reality

Title: *Amos Alligator Arrives at the Airport*
Author: Janice Sinclair
Genre: Picture Book
Format: Paperback Book works with an application to augment the
    presented text.
URL: https://alivestudiosco.com/storybooksalive
Cost: Less than $10.00 per copy

Participant Materials

*   Copy of *Amos Alligator Arrives at the Airport*

Facilitator Materials

*   Access to the application
*   Device to run the application

Standards Alignment

AASL: I
ISTE: 1

Description

Amos Alligator Arrives at the Airport is an interactive story that comes to life by an augmented text experience when used in combination with an application. The downloadable Storybooks alive application does contain highlighted text, audio, and animation.

Activities

The one-to-one read-aloud experience is a wonderful way to engage the augmented reality text. Amos and all his friends materialize on your device and interact with your Pre-K reader as they touch the screen. This book is perfect for one-to-one guided read-aloud. It allows the student to have control of the resource and the facilitator to be in a supportive role to help guide the Pre-K student through the narrative. This text does contain augmentations that could be seen as enabling or disabling toward guiding through the text for comprehension purposes. The one-to-one participant experience would be immersive and engaging.

Dynamic Dialogue

Title: *Robot Zot*
Author: Jon Scieszka
Genre: Picture Book
Format: Online Epic! Book
URL: https://www.getepic.com/app/read/14220
Cost: Free

Participant Materials

- Copy of *Robot Zot*

Facilitator Materials

- Access to the application
- Device to run the application
- Method of projection will be the smart board

Standards Alignment

AASL: III
ISTE: 1

Description

Robot Zot is about to attack Earth! Zot goes through much to arrive on Earth. Should we be scared of the robot arrival? What should we do? Wait for the twist of fortune. This version of the book *Robot Zot* has limited visual and voice.

Activities

The large group read-aloud with augmented reality allows for the facilitator to guide the participant experience. It requires a single copy of the transmedia text to be used to serve an entire group of participants. The use of a single resource can make this a cost-effective option for facilitators. Then the digital read-aloud can transition to small group activity. Participants can share what they would do with Robot Zot. It allows the facilitator to have control of the experience and still allow for participant discussion. The small group participant experience would be communal and allow for greater discussion of the resource content.

Elementary School

Augmented Reality

Title: *An Elephant in Our Garden*
Author: Patrick E. McLeod
Genre: Picture Book
Format: Paperback Book works with an application to augment the presented text
URL: https://books.google.com/books/about/An_Elephant_in_Our_Garden.html?id=GEEBng EACAAJ&source=kp_book_description
Cost: Under $10.00 per copy

Participant Materials

- Copy of *An Elephant in Our Garden*
- Paper and crayons

Facilitator Materials

- Access to the application and book.
- Device for use will be the iPad.

Standards Alignment

AASL: III
ISTE: 1

Description

The vegetables in the garden are being eaten. Isabella imagines that it might be an elephant or a bear or even a penguin. Follow along in this who-done-it mystery using her imagination and logic. The cover and four interior pages of this book have augmented reality. Bring them to life with your iPad and an Internet connection.

Activities

The large group read-aloud with augmented reality gives the facilitator the opportunity to share the visual experience of the augmented reality through the use of pairing the iPad with a projection screen. It requires a single copy of the augmented reality. The use of a single resource can make this a cost-effective option for facilitators. At the conclusion of the digital read-aloud portion the participants can be encouraged to use paper and crayons to create a visual of what might be in their garden eating vegetables.

Dynamic Dialogue

Title: *Sid the Science Kid: The Trouble with Germs*
Author: PBS Kids
Genre: Fiction/Informational
Format: eBook
URL: http://pbskids.org/apps/sid-the-science-kid-the-trouble-with-germs.html
Cost: Free

Participant Materials

- Copy of *Sid the Science Kid: The Trouble with Germs*

Facilitator Materials

- Access to the webpage via computer.
- Device of computer will be used.
- Method of projection will be the smart board.

Standards Alignment

AASL: I
ISTE: 1

Description

Sid discovers why he has to wash his hands to get rid of germs. Sid can't see the germs, so his mom shows him a picture through a powerful microscope that shows those tiny things do exist and can make him sick. The eBook contains highlighted text and audio to guide reading.

Activities

The large group read-aloud guided by the facilitator will work well for *Sid the Science Kid: The Trouble with Germs*. The eBook text will be paused to allow for discussion and group questioning to impact discussion. In order to maximize participant group engagement and discussion the choice of dynamic dialog will only require a single copy of the dynamic dialog text to be used to serve an entire group of participants. The use of a single resource can make this a cost-effective option for facilitators.

Middle School

Augmented Reality

Title: *Red Cell White Cell: A STEM Based Children's Book*
Author: Michael Brown
Genre: Informational
Format: Application
URL: https://www.amazon.com/Red-Cell-White-childrens-featuring-ebook
  /dp/B00IMNJQ1Q
Cost: Less than $10.00 per copy

Participant Materials

* Copy of *Red Cell White Cell: A STEM Based Children's Book*

Facilitator Materials

* Access the application and have the hard copy book.
* Device for use would be the iPad.

Standards Alignment

AASL: III
ISTE: 1

Description

Teach your children about the basic functions of blood cells using literature. Using augmented reality, watch the 3D model appear.

Activities

The one-to-one read-aloud experience is a method by which to engage the augmented reality text. It allows the student to have control of the resource and be supported by the facilitator. The one-to-one participant experience is optimal with augmented reality texts of this nature.

The small group read-aloud is perfect for a moderately participant-controlled experience of augmented reality. It allows the facilitator to have control of the resource and direct the participant experience. The small group participant experience can be with one book and iPad with the added benefit of group discussion element.

The large group read-aloud with augmented reality allows for the facilitator to guide the participant experience. It requires a single copy of the augmented reality text to be used to serve an entire group of participants. The use of a single resource can make this a cost-effective option for facilitators.

Dynamic Dialogue

Title: *Children of Time*
Author: Adrian Tchaikovksy
Genre: Science Fiction
Format: Audio Book
URL: https://www.amazon.com/Children-of-Time/dp/B06ZXTHNSJ/ref
 =tmm_aud_swatch_0
Cost: Less than $20.00 per copy

Participant Materials

- Copy of *Children of Time*

Facilitator Materials

- Access the application and have the hard copy book.
- Device for use would be the iPad.

Standards Alignment

AASL: II
ISTE: 1

Description

A struggle has begun for the new Earth. Testing the boundaries of what they will do to survive. This transmedia material is an audio book.

Activity

The one-to-one read-aloud experience is a positive way to engage the dynamic dialog text. It allows the student to have control of the resource and the facilitator to be in a supportive role. The one-to-one participant experience would be immersive.

The small group read-aloud is perfect for using Audible. It allows the facilitator to be in a passive role. The small group participant experience can be communal and self-directed with appropriate precorrection.

The large group read-aloud with dynamic dialogue through Audible allows for the facilitator to guide the participant experience. It would be positive to extend the experience by allowing a visual drawing response.

High School

Augmented Reality

Title: *Border wall is a recipe for ecosystem disaster, park conservationists say.*
Author: By Los Angeles Times, adapted by Newsela staff
Genre: Informational
Format: Online Periodical
URL: www.newsela.com
Cost: Free

Participant Materials

- Copy on the level of each participant of *Border wall is a recipe for ecosystem disaster, park conservationists say*

Facilitator Materials

- Access via the web application.
- Device could be an iPad or computer.
- As needed access to a printer for copies.

Standards Alignment

AASL: II
ISTE: 1

Description:

Online article *Border wall is a recipe for ecosystem disaster, park conservationists say* is one of many articles present on Newsela. Newsela provides articles of varied difficulty level to meet participant need. This can have a positive impact on the digital read-aloud experience, allowing the facilitator to select levels for personalized learning.

Activities

This transmedia resource could be addressed by one-to-one, small group, or large group means based on the need for engaging the text. The one-to-one read-aloud experience is a wonderful way to engage the digital dialogue text. It allows the student to have control of the resource and the facilitator to be in a supportive role. The one-to-one participant experience would allow for time to read and reread materials.

The small group read-aloud is a perfect vehicle for the shared reading experience. It allows for a more advanced reader to work with and scaffold a challenged reader. In the shared reading both participants take turns reading and engaging with the digital dialogue.

The large group read-aloud with augmented reality allows for the facilitator to guide the participant experience. It requires a single copy of the augmented reality text to be used to serve an entire group of participants. The use of a single resource can make this a cost-effective option for facilitators.

Dynamic Dialogue

Title: *Explorer Academy: The Nebula Effect*

Author: Trudi Trueit

Genre: Science/Adventure

Format: Transmedia book

URL: https://www.amazon.com/Explorer-Academy-Nebula-Trudi-Trueit/dp/1426331592/ref=sr_1_1_sspa

Cost: Under $15.00 per copy

Participant Materials

- Copy of *Explorer Academy: The Nebula Effect*

Facilitator Materials

- A computer for access to the online components.
- Device could be an iPad or Computer.

Standards Alignment

AASL: V

ISTE: 3

Description

The book has embedded excitement with puzzles and codes embedded throughout. The online components can be accessed through the Internet. The book can be used stand-alone or as a combination experience.

Activities

The explorers in this adventure text aren't alone. Participants can get involved by engaging in the online functions. The large group read-aloud experience can spark discussion of the text and function elements. The text allows for the facilitator to guide the participants' experience. It requires a single copy of the augmented reality text to be used to serve an entire group of participants.

Lifelong Learner

Story Author

<u>Digital Resource</u>

Title: Dot and Dash

Format: Robots and applications that allow for coding

Description: Authors can create their own dynamic dialogues and experiences while coding the robots.

URL: www.makewonder.com

Cost: The robot is under $200.00 and the applications are free.

Standards Alignment

AASL: VI

ISTE: 6

Activity

Dash to Read a Book

Participants will engage with coding and computer science to create a transmedia talk. Participants will select a favorite transmedia.

Participants will write a paragraph summary of the transmedia.

Participants will use the paragraph to record into Dot or Dash to create a Transmedia Book Talk.

<u>Materials Needed:</u>

- We will be using Dot and/or Dash.

- These Transmedia Book Talks will be used to create a recorded dialogue using the coding robots Dot, Dash, and the Go computer application.

- Computer for research as needed.

<u>Your Tasks:</u>

1. In groups, choose the book to create a Transmedia Book Talk to support.
2. In your group, use the selected transmedia material to create a descriptive paragraph.
3. Create your own recordings on the iPad using the Go application.
4. In your groups make sure to test the robots to ensure the recording can be heard and understood.
5. Prepare to perform your book talk.

Code Author

Title: *I Survived This Story*

Format: Application

Description: *Audacity* is an open source web-based program developed to use for the creation of multitrack recordings. The participants will draw on personal experience, research, or shared knowledge to create a story about surviving during a storm. When the code-like tracks are layered together correctly, the story emerges. The application allows for cut, copy, splice, and mix.

URL: www.audacityteam.org

Cost: Free open source code

Standards Alignment

AASL: IV

ISTE: 3

Activity

I Survived This Story

Using Audacity to create a story of storm survival. The participants can engage individually, dyads, or small groups. The Audacity web-based download will be able to record multiple tracks to allow for individual character recording. The layering of these tracks correctly with a music track will set the scene and create a well coded striped story. We will facilitate student agency, and the facilitator role will be that of a project manager. The facilitator engages only as needed to redirect, allowing students to be self-directed and use their participant agency.

<u>Resources/Materials Needed:</u>

- Computer
- Audacity

<u>Your Task:</u>

1. Through the use of personal or shared creativity:
    a. Isolate a storm experience to use for your audio story coding with Audacity.
    b. Write and code how and where the sound stripes will need to connect to create the optimal story experience for the participant listeners.
    c. Record the voice strands and decide how the storm sounds will be represented.

Introduce Audacity and demonstrate to the participants how to download the application. Then create a simple recording using multiple track strands and visually demonstrate how the strands can be moved to shape the story. Share a premade example of the *I Survived This Story* to allow for an auditory experience from which to build creativity. The use of Audacity and the creation of a storm story will allow for personal expression and a greater understanding of weather phenomena.

Student Activities

Participants will:
- Load and open Audacity.
- Use personal, researched, or shared experiences to create the storm story.

- Participants should write their story stripes that will be recorded and moved to maximize the impact of the storm story.
- Each participant or group of participants should then record the story stripes.
- Once recorded the story stripes should be coded into an arrangement that allows for an impactive storytelling.
- The completed story will then be shared with the group. This will allow for participants to be the leaders of the digital storytelling and the facilitator role to be secondary.

This activity is inspired by the *I Survived . . .* book series and allows for the scientific experience of learning about weather phenomena to be a personal experience. There are many different books in the series. The complex exploration and problem solving required to create the story, audio, and present may lend itself to multiple sessions or a group experience.

Conclusion

This creative confluence between science and coding highlights what can be when you use cross-curricular engagement and think outside the book to power up your read-alouds with technology. Scientific learning can be enhanced through the use of quality literature and the opportunities present in coding.

CHAPTER NINE

History/Social Studies

History and social studies have endorsed the use of both books and transmedia literature to learn about content. Transmedia literature can open doors to experiencing other cultures through a genuine human experience found in history and social studies. This can be accomplished through literature, allowing participants to make meaningful connections between information and the real world. History and social studies can offer participants problems that are at once connected to their lives and have no clear solution, so in this way encouraging critical thinking skills and expression of points of view (Harb 2007).

The history/social studies materials and read-aloud activities listed reflect examples implemented to demonstrate the many available resources within the category and in multiple formats. It is possible for each of these and others in this resource category to be a stand-alone, read-aloud text experience, creator experience, or be supplemented with a more personalized experience. It also has the potential to be a technology-enhanced delivery by using the varied applications. These applications are designed to support history/social studies learning through reading experiences and otherwise. The resources can be delivered with a single child, small group, or large group activity.

The following is a Materials section designed to give hands-on practical application examples to support success of implementation. All of the transmedia materials highlighted in this section are categorized for Pre-K, Elementary, Middle, and High, then comprised of Augmented Reality and Dynamic Dialogue that consists of Title, Author, Genre, Format, URL, Cost, Participant Materials, Facilitator Materials, Standards Alignment, Description, and Activities. The Lifelong Learner section focuses on Story Author and Code Author experiences.

Pre-K

Augmented Reality

Title: *Don't Let the Pigeon Drive This App*
Author: Mo Willems
Genre: Transmedia
Format: Application
URL: https://itunes.apple.com/us/app/dont-let-pigeon-run-this-app
     /id459749670?mt=8
Cost: Under $10.00 per copy

Participant Materials

* Copy of *Don't Let the Pigeon Drive This App*

Facilitator Materials

* Access through iTunes as a downloadable application.
* Device used would be an iPad.
* Method of delivery will be through a smart board.

Standards Alignment

AASL: I
ISTE: 1

Description

Mo Willems brings our beloved Pigeon to a transmedia digital screen time near you with this application loaded with functions.

Activities

The one-to-one and small group read-aloud experience is the optimal way to engage the augmented reality text. It allows the student to have personalized learning experience. The participant experience would allow for student decision making and voice in delivery. It gives the facilitator acting in the role of coach to have the ability to serve multiple individuals during the digital read-aloud without drastically impacting the personalization of the learning experience. The participant experience would be communal and allow for greater discussion of the resource content.

Dynamic Dialogue

Title: *Applesauce Season*
Author: Eden Ross Lipson
Genre: Picture Book
Format: Audible Audio Book
URL: https://www.amazon.com/Applesauce-Season/dp/B00CUIV824/ref
   =sr_1_1
Cost: Less than $10.00 per copy

Participant Materials

- Copy of *Applesauce Season*

Facilitator Materials

- Access to the audio will be established through Audible.
- Device used can be an iPad.
- Audio book will play, and the Elmo will be used to display the physical book visually.

Standards Alignment

AASL: I
ISTE: 1

Description

This is a traditional book that has an audio version that can be accessed for sharing dynamic dialogue.

Activities

The one-to-one, small group, and large group dynamic dialogue read-aloud experience can be further engaged by using repeated reading. Allow the audio to play to an agreed upon point in the text and then pause. The participant then rereads the materials aloud with the support of the facilitator. It allows the student to have control of the resource and the facilitator to be in a supportive role. It allows the facilitator to direct the participant experience with a focus on supportive reading guidance. The participant experience would be communal and allow for greater discussion of the resource content.

Elementary School

Augmented Reality

Title: *If I Ran for President*
Author: Catherine Stier
Genre: Picture Book
Format: Video or Book Reading and traditional book
URL: https://www.storylineonline.net/books/if-i-ran-for-president
Cost: Under $10.00 for the book and the web reading of the book is free.

Participant Materials

- Copy of *If I Ran for President*

Facilitator Materials

- Access to the Internet with web browser.
- Device to use would be an iPad.
- Method of whole group delivery is via smart board.

Standards Alignment

AASL: I
ISTE: 1

Description

Imagine all of the hard work you would need to do to be president and the complex problems you would need to solve. If you ran for president, you would need to study the nation's problems, tell the American people about your platform, select a running mate, and debate your opponents on live television.

Activities

The large group digital read-aloud experience is a wonderful way to engage the augmented reality text. It can allow the participant and facilitator to have joint control of the resource and the facilitator to be in a coach style role. The video providing dynamic dialogue allows for shared facilitation that can be participant controlled with facilitator guidance. The participant experience will be guided but still have participant facilitators and group interaction through targeted experience support with the dynamic dialogue resource.

Dynamic Dialogue

Title: *Curiosityville China*
Author: Houghton Mifflin Harcourt.
Genre: Informational
Format: Transmedia
URL: https://www.curiosityville.com/pablo-welcome-video/
Cost: Limited free subscription

Participant Materials

- Copy of *Curiosityville China*

Facilitator Materials

- Access through webpage and the Internet.
- Device will use the computer to increase functionality.
- Method of delivery will be using the overhead projector and multiple participant presenters.

Standard Alignment

AASL: I
ISTE: 1

Description

Curiosityville China is a multimedia application for learning that provides cultural information related to many countries.

Activities

The digital read-aloud experience can engage participants in the transmedia material in a multitude of ways. The selected method will be participant presenter. Each of the participants will take turns leading the group through the website. This will allow for all participants to have brains-on and hands-on experience. When using an application, it is important to use the method that will reach the maximum number of participants and share the transmedia material in the most effective manner.

Middle School

Augmented Reality

Title: *Egypt (Great Civilisations)*
Author: Eva Bargallo
Genre: Information/History
Format: Augmented Reality Text
URL: https://www.amazon.com/Egypt-Great-Civilisations-Eva-Bargall%C3
%B3/dp/191059685X/ref=pd_ybh_a_47
Cost: Less than $10.00 per copy

Participant Materials

*   Copy of *Egypt (Great Civilisations)*

Facilitator Materials

*   Access to the application.
*   Device will be an iPad.
*   Method will be mirrored iPad with smart board.

Standards Alignment

AASL: I
ISTE: 1

Description

Egyptian civilization was a culture that was outstanding not only for its impressive artistic and architectural works. This book, complete with augmented reality features, will shed light on Egypt's empire for young and curious minds.

Activities

The one-to-one read-aloud experience is an engaging way to encounter the augmented reality text. It allows the student to have control of the resource and the facilitator to be in a supportive role of a coach demonstrating positive feedback but ultimately supporting from the sidelines.

The small group read-aloud allows the facilitator to have control of the resource and direct the participant experience. The small group participant experience would be communal and allow for greater discussion of the resource content.

The large group read-aloud with augmented reality allows for the facilitator to address the participants' technology knowledge and aid them in how to navigate an augmented reality text through modeling of best practices. It requires a single copy of the augmented reality text to be used to serve an entire group of participants. The use of a single resource can make this a cost-effective option for facilitators.

Dynamic Dialogue

Title: *Helen of Troy*
Author: StoryNory
Genre: History
Format: Webpage
URL: https://www.storynory.com/helen-of-troy
Cost: Free

Participant Materials

- Selected resource is a webpage.

Facilitator Materials

- Access to the webpage.
- Device will be computer based.

Standards Alignment

AASL: I
ISTE: 1

Description

StoryNory is a website that gives short but impactful descriptions of stories. They are narrations and have text in a supportive role. The story *Helen of Troy* follows this format and can be very helpful for first-time, simple transmedia encounter with the story.

Activities

The digital read-aloud experience with *Helen of Troy* is quite straightforward. It is a website with digital dialogue. This is an efficient and effective way to engage this complex story simply with transmedia text. It allows the facilitator or participant to have control of the resource.

High School

Augmented Reality

Title: *Rediscovering the blazingly bright colors of ancient sculptures*
Author: Atlas Obscura, adapted by Newsela staff
Genre: Informational/Social Sciences
Format: Transmedia
URL: www.newsela.net
Cost: Free subscription

Participant Materials

- Copy of *Rediscovering the blazingly bright colors of ancient sculptures*

Facilitator Materials

- Access via the web application.
- Device used could be an iPad or computer.
- Method of delivery would be through the smart board.

Standards Alignment

AASL: IV
ISTE: 3

Description

Online article at high school level about *Rediscovering the blazingly bright colors of ancient sculptures* from the Atlas Obscura, adapted by Newsela staff.

Activities

This activity will be for a large group digital read-aloud with Atlas Obscura, adapted by Newsela staff, and allows for the participant to guide the experience. It requires a smart board screen be used to serve an entire group of participants. The participants will take turns being the facilitator and deliver alternating pages. The facilitator will be in the role of project manager supervising logistics but not interfering with the participant delivery of content.

Dynamic Dialogue

Title: *Jack Hunter and the French Connection*
Author: Martin King
Genre: Mystery
Format: Book with application
URL: https://www.amazon.com/Jack-Hunter-French-Connection-Martin/dp /0957102119
Cost: Less than $25.00 per copy

Participant Materials

- Copy of *Jack Hunter and the French Connection*

Facilitator Materials

- Access via the Internet to the application.
- Device used will be the iPad.
- Method.

Standards Alignment

AASL: I
ISTE: 1

Description

Mystery and intrigue along with 3D interaction and a game.

Activities

The one-to-one read-aloud experience is the optimal way to engage the augmented reality text. It allows the participant to have control of the resource and the facilitator to be in a supportive role. The one-to-one participant experience would be immersive and requires little guidance.

The small group read-aloud is perfect for targeted experience with guidance. It allows the facilitator to maintain attention. The small group participant experience would be communal and allows for greater discussion of the resource content.

The large group read-aloud has the group dynamic to help produce engaging discussions. It requires a single copy of the augmented reality text to be used to serve an entire group of participants. The use of a single resource can make this a cost-effective option for facilitators.

Lifelong Learner

Story Author

Digital Resource

Title: Comic Life

Format: Web Application

Description: Authors can create their own transmedia dynamic dialogues using Comic Life.

URL: http://plasq.com/apps/comiclife/macwin

Cost: The website has a free trial.

Standards Alignment

AASL: IV

ISTE: 6

Activity

Pressing Issues in History

Participants will engage with the following topics and create an original comic story to share with their group.

- Explain how books were made and ideas communicated prior to the invention of Gutenberg's movable-type printing press.

- Describe how the movable type works.

- Explain how the invention of the printing press changed what information was distributed and how.

- Explain how this shift in information spurred cultural change.

<u>*Materials Needed:*</u>

- We will need paper and pencil to do the layout for the Comic Life submission.

- The website access to Comic Life.

- Computer for research.

<u>*Your Tasks:*</u>

Instruct students to use the application Comic Life to create a comic book history of the impact of the movable-type printing press. The comic book should include the following:

- Three pages in chronological order with at least three panels on each page.

- An appropriate picture in each panel, including the source URL.

- Captions and speech or thought bubble(s) for each photo.

- At least three big ideas about before, during, and after the invention of the press, taken from notes.

This creation of the comic panel enables participants to have a virtual literary maker moment. The participants are able to create their own story and then be the facilitator and share their work with others in their groups. In between history and literature this highlights one option of what can be when you use cross-curricular engagement to power up our student maker agency.

Code Author

Title: *Tynker with Maps*

Format: Application

Description: *Tynker* is a coding application that allows for multiple levels of cross-curricular engagement. It is described as coding made easy. The platform can be used on multiple devices and be embedded within our gaming platforms such as Minecraft. Tynker employs a drag and drop coding style.

URL: www.tynker.com

Cost: Varies depending on version and functions

Standards Alignment

AASL: VI

ISTE: 6

Activity

Tynker with Maps

Use Tynker to create a map of a story location. We will facilitate student agency, and the facilitator role will be that of a project manager. The facilitator engages individual students only as needed to redirect, allowing students to be self-directed and use their participant agency.

Resources/Materials Needed:

- Computer
- Tynker.com

Your Task:

1. Through exploration:
   a. Select a location from a story to map.
   b. Analyze the location and decipher which landforms are present and need to be included.
   c. Understand that the included landforms will be layered on the map.
   d. Decide in which order the landforms should be placed on the map.

Introduce the concept of deciphering fictional landscapes with the assistance of landforms. Show to participants how you can use materials available in Tynker to create the layers and assemble the map. Explain to participants that they will be presenting the story scene and the landform map with a verbal description to the group as a digital storytelling.

Student Activities

Participants will:
- Load and open Tynker.
- Use the following landforms to create a map of a fictional location from a story.
  - Hill
  - Island
  - Ocean

- Mountain
- Desert
- River

- Participants should record the landforms and how they will be layered in the creation process.
- Each participant should then be able to demonstrate the layering of the parts and describe as a story with an introduction that highlights the chosen story.

This activity is adapted from materials shared on the Tynker.com website. They have many lesson plans that are from across the curriculum and can be cross-curricular in application. By anchoring the participant in the story, participants will be encouraged to share their results as a digital storytelling.

Conclusion

History and social studies joint use of transmedia literature, to learn about content, can spark heightened interest in both topics. Transmedia literature can capture moments of the human condition and existence, then display them digitally for participants to enjoy. This can allow for meaningful real-world connections to be forged with content. History and social studies can offer participants challenges that will shape their view of humanity and the world (Harb 2007).

CHAPTER TEN

Visual Performing Arts

The visual performing arts materials and read-aloud activities listed reflect multiple offerings implemented to demonstrate the many options available. Each of these and others in this resource category can be a stand-alone, read-aloud text experience, creator experience, or personalized learning. It also has the potential to be a technology-enhanced delivery by using the varied applications. The applications are designed to engage participants in the visual performing arts through reading-aloud and exploration extension activities. The resources can be implemented with a single child, small group, or large group activity.

The following is a Materials section designed to give hands-on practical application examples to support success implementation. All of the transmedia materials highlighted in this section are categorized for Pre-K, Elementary, Middle, and High, then comprised of Augmented Reality and Dynamic Dialogue that consists of Title, Author, Genre, Format, URL, Cost, Participant Materials, Facilitator Materials, Standards Alignment, Description, and Activities. The Lifelong Learner section focuses on Story Author and Code Author experiences.

Pre-K

Augmented Reality

Title: *ABC Animals Alphabet*

Author: Sarina Simon

Genre: Picture Book

Format: Paperback Book works with an application to augment the presented text.

URL: https://itunes.apple.com/us/app/abc-animals-ar/id1140627076?mt=8

Cost: Under $15.00 per copy

Participant Materials

- Copy of *ABC Animals Alphabet*

Facilitator Materials

- Access to the Internet and the application.
- Device for use with iPad.
- Method of digital read-aloud delivery will be mirrored iPad to smart board.

Standards Alignment

AASL: I

ISTE: 1

Description

A paperback book working with an application to augment the presented text, walking you through the alphabet on an animal journey.

Activities

The one-to-one read-aloud is an efficient way to work with Pre-K participants, who need guidance as they engage the augmented reality text. It can be frustrating to use the applications if you have not had an opportunity to learn. The one-on-one format allows the participant to have control of the resource and the facilitator to be in a strongly supportive role. The one-to-one participant experience would be immersive.

The small group read-aloud is excellent for a less immersive but still intense level of aid with how to work with the augmented reality resource. It allows the facilitator to support control of the resource and direct the participant experience. The small group participant experience would be communal and allows for greater discussion of the resource content.

The large group read-aloud with augmented reality allows for the facilitator to model the proper use of iPad during the experience. It requires a single copy of the augmented reality text to be used to serve an entire group of participants. The use of a single resource can make this a cost-effective option for facilitators.

Dynamic Dialogue

Title: *Good Night Moon for iPad*
Author: Margaret Wise Brown
Genre: Picture Book
Format: Application
URL: https://itunes.apple.com/us/app/goodnight-moon-a-classic-bedtime
-storybook/id546560960?mt=8
Cost: Under $5.00 per copy

Participant Materials

- Copy of *Good Night Moon for iPad*

Facilitator Materials

- Access to the Internet and the application.
- Device for use with iPad.
- Method of digital read-aloud delivery will be mirrored iPad to smart board.

Standards Alignment

AASL: I
ISTE: 1

Description

The children's classic *Goodnight Moon* was created and now has been beautifully reimagined as an interactive app designed for your iPod.

Activities

The large group read-aloud with transmedia can be exciting and challenging. Pre-K patrons are generally disappointed if they cannot have hands-on interaction. It may be appropriate to do precorrection about when, how, and why participants may engage with the technology. This allows for the facilitator to guide the participant experience and aid in comfortable understanding. It requires a single copy of the augmented reality text to be used to serve an entire group of participants. The use of a single resource can make this a cost-effective option for facilitators.

Elementary School

Augmented Reality

Title: *Ernie's Wish Trail*
Author: Maia Orion
Genre: Picture Book
Format: Paperback Book works with an application to augment the
    presented text.
URL: https://www.abebooks.com/9780996926409/Ernies-Wish-Trail
    -Interactive Childrens-0996926402/plp
Cost: Less than $15.00 per copy

Participant Materials

- Copy of *Ernie's Wish Trail*

Facilitator Materials

- Access to the Internet and the application.
- Device for use with iPad.
- Method of digital read-aloud delivery will be mirrored iPad to smart board.

Standards Alignment

AASL: I
ISTE: 1

Description

Ernie's Wish Trail is a book enabled for augmented reality with an application. In every interaction Ernie has a new wish to be someone else and possessing their natural gifts. Ernie's wish trail ends in rediscovering simple pleasures and the joys of being himself.

Activities

The one-to-one read-aloud experience is an excellent way to engage the augmented reality text. It allows the student to have control of the resource and the facilitator to be in a supportive role. The one-to-one participant experience would be immersive.

The small group read-aloud is immersive but still has the social experience of the large group. It allows the facilitator to have control of the resource and direct the participant experience. The small group participant experience would be communal and allows for greater discussion of the resource content.

The large group read-aloud with augmented reality allows for the facilitator to guide the participant experience. It requires a single copy of the augmented reality text to be used to serve an entire group of participants. The use of a single resource can make this a cost-effective option for facilitators.

Dynamic Dialogue

Title: *The Day the Crayons Quit*
Author: Drew Daywalt
Genre: Picture Book
Format: eBook
URL: https://www.barnesandnoble.com/w/the-day-the-crayons-quit-drew
-daywalt/1113054468?type=eBook
Cost: Less than $15.00 per copy

Participant Materials

- Selected resource is a Kindle book.

Facilitator Materials

- To access the Kindle book, would need wifi unless downloaded.
- Device would need to be Kindle.

Standards Alignment

AASL: I
ISTE: 1

Description

Duncan just wants to color. His crayons have had enough! They quit!

Activity

The one-to-one read-aloud experience is with an eBook through the Kindle. It allows the student to have control of the resource and the facilitator to be in a supportive role. The one-to-one participant experience would be immersive.

The small group read-aloud works well with all of the participants having a Kindle and downloaded book. It allows the facilitator to have control of the resource and direct the participant experience. The small group participant experience would be communal and allows for greater discussion of the resource content.

Middle School

Augmented Reality

Title: *The Mischievians*
Author: William Joyce
Genre: Picture Book
Format: eBook
URL: https://www.amazon.com/Mischievians-William-Joyce/dp/1442473
    479/ref=sr_1_1
Cost: Less than $15.00 per copy

Participant Materials

- Copy of *The Mischievians*

Facilitator Materials

- To access the Kindle book, would need wifi unless downloaded.
- Device would need to be Kindle.
- Method would be whole group Kindle read.

Standards Alignment

AASL: V
ISTE: 3

Description

Lost something or break something? It's not your fault—blame the Mischievians.

Activities

The one-to-one read-aloud experience with the Kindle is optimal. It allows the student to have control of the resource and the facilitator to be in a supportive role. The one-to-one participant experience would be immersive.

The small group read-aloud can work well for the Kindle, allowing the facilitator to read aloud while the participants follow along silently. It allows the facilitator to have control of the resource and direct the participant experience. The small group participant experience would be communal and allows for greater discussion of the resource content.

The large group read-aloud with Kindle allows for the facilitator to guide the participant experience as a coach circulating with positive feedback and tips for screen reading success.

Dynamic Dialogue

Title: *A Bean Stalk and a Boy Named Jack*
Author: William Joyce
Genre: Picture Book
Format: eBook Augments with additional functions
URL: http://www.simonandschuster.com/books/A-Bean-a-Stalk-and-a-Boy
     -Named-Jack/William-Joyce/9781442473492
Cost: Less than $20.00 per copy

Participant Materials

- Copy of *A Bean Stalk and a Boy Named Jack*

Facilitator Materials

- Access to the eBook would require Internet for downloading.
- Device would be the iPad.
- Method would be to use a mirrored iPad and a smart board.

Standards Alignment

AASL: I
ISTE: 1

Description

This a twist on the old story we all know brought into the present day with eBook applications.

Activities

The one-to-one read-aloud experience is a wonderful way to engage the augmented reality text. It allows the student to have control of the resource and the facilitator to be in a supportive role. It can also be full of disabling distractors. Working closely with middle-school-aged participants as they read the eBook will help them learn how to get the most out of transmedia. The one-to-one participant experience would be immersive.

The small group read-aloud is perfect for a less immersive but still targeted experience of the dynamic dialogue resource. It allows the facilitator to have control of the resource and direct the participant experience. The small group participant experience would be communal and allows for greater discussion of the resource content.

The large group read-aloud with augmented reality allows for the facilitator to guide the participant experience. It requires a single copy of the augmented reality text to be used to serve an entire group of participants. The use of a single resource can make this a cost-effective option for facilitators.

High School

Augmented Reality

Title: *Steam Whistle Alley: An Adventure in Augmented Reality*
Author: Joshua Mason
Genre: Science Fiction
Format: eBook
URL: https://www.barnesandnoble.com/w/steam-whistle-alley-joshua
   -mason/1129119494
Cost: Less than $20.00 per copy

Participant Materials

- Copy of *Steam Whistle Alley: An Adventure in Augmented Reality*

Facilitator Materials

- Access to the book and application.
- Device would be an iPad for access to the eBook.
- Method would be for everyone to have a copy of the book and have a group read and Literary LARP.

Standards Alignment

AASL: I
ISTE: 1

Description

A thrilling new entry into the science fiction genres, Steam Whistle Alley combines gaming mechanics with aesthetics through the magic of advanced augmented reality.

Activities

The one-to-one read-aloud experience is a way to engage the augmented reality and live action role play. It allows the student to have control of the resource and the facilitator to be in a supportive role. The one-to-one participant experience would be immersive.

The small group read-aloud is perfect for a less immersive but still targeted experience of the augmented reality resource. It allows the facilitator to have control of the resource and direct the participant experience. The small group participant experience would be communal and allows for greater discussion of the resource content.

The large group read-aloud with augmented reality allows for the facilitator to guide the participant experience. It requires multiple copies of the augmented reality text to be used to serve an entire group of participants.

Dynamic Dialogue

Title: *Hero of Thera: A LitRPG Novel*
Author: Eric Nylund
Genre: Science Fiction
Format: eBook
URL: https://www.amazon.com/Hero-Thera-LitRPG-Eric-Nylund-ebook/dp/B0719CYNCG
Cost: Less than $15.00 per copy

Participant Materials

- Selected resource and Internet access

Facilitator Materials

- Access to the book and application.
- Device would be an iPad for access to the eBook.

Standards Alignment

AASL: I
ISTE: 1

Description

This is a literature role-playing game eBook.

The one-to-one read-aloud experience would work well as it comes in hardback and an eBook with additional functionalities. The small group read-aloud would be optimal as it comes in hardback and an eBook with additional functionalities that make it a literature role-playing game. It allows the facilitator to have control of the resource and direct the participant experience. The small group participant experience would be communal and allows for greater discussion of the resource content.

The large group read-aloud would work well as it comes in hardback and an eBook with additional functionalities that create the literary role-playing aspect of the experience.

Lifelong Learner

Story Author

Title: *Flip That Story*

Format: Website or download

Description: Participants can become authors by creating their own stories, adding text and other visuals to a Word document.

URL: fliphtml5.com

Cost: Free version available with limited functionality

Standards Alignment

AASL: VI
ISTE: 6

Activity

Flip That Story

eMagazines takes storytelling and engages a palette of technical tools available within a Word document. The participants will be using images, graphics, music, and sound mixed together with the participant author's own story voice. We will allow our participants the ultimate expression of creativity, the creation of an original piece of literature that is shared during the digital read-aloud experience.

<u>Resources/Materials Needed:</u>

- Computer
- Curriculum documents
- Fliphtml5.com

<u>Your Task:</u>

You will create a digital story with at least 10 eMagazine pages on your authentic topic. Be sure to review your written content before you create your project and again before you submit your project.

1. Determine how you are going to access the eMagazine application.
2. Decide on the story you want to tell.
3. Write your story script.
4. Create a storyboard.
5. Create your digital story with the following elements:
   a. Include at least 10 eMagazine pages. You may need more than 10 eMagazine pages to make a complete story.
   b. Create a title screen at the beginning of your eMagazine story.
   c. Edit your digital eMagazine pages if needed.
6. Share the finished product in a participant-led digital read-aloud. When completed reflect on your process and how it works to have a participant presenter.
   a. How did the Fliphtml5 application work for the digital eMagazine?
   b. What technical problems did you encounter when creating this project?
   c. How did you use this eMagazine pages storytelling in your digital read-aloud?

Code Author

<u>Digital Resource</u>

Title: Dot and Dash

Format: Coding Application and Robots

Description: Code authors can create their own coded dialogue about
their favorite picture.

URL: www.makewonder.com

Cost: The applications are free; the Robots are less than $200.

Standards Alignment

AASL: VI

ISTE: 6

Activity

Talk about Art

Participants will engage with the following topics and create an original robot dialogue about art with their partner.

- Select your favorite work of art. This can be done from print, eBooks, or any transmedia materials present.
- Collect three facts about your work of art.
- Make sure the three facts are short in nature.
- Discuss with your partner the different works for art chosen.

<u>Materials Needed:</u>

- We will need paper and pencil to write out the facts about your favorite work of art.
- Two Dash robots.
- Two iPads.

<u>Your Tasks:</u>

Instruct participants to use the applications Go and Blockly to accomplish the following tasks. The final product should include the following:

- Open the Go application and speak your questions into the recorder.
- Open the Blockly application and code the two robots with "if" and "when" commands designed to facilitate the robots talking.
- Make the recorded questions part of the coding of the robots.
- Dot and Dash will be coded to react and discuss art based on your learning.

This creation of the robot dialogue about art is to engage participants in a cross-curricular experience that involves art, coding, and writing. The participants are able to create their own dialogue and then be the facilitator and share their work with others in their group.

Conclusion

Allow for the possibility that transmedia materials deliberately selected for literature quality can encourage visualization of events and connections to participants' lives, as they connect with prior knowledge on the topic. These created connections can be the vehicle for creative thinking by allowing opportunities for new learning and increasing the link between fictional representations and transmedia, informational text. Participants can develop an opinion and learn to demonstrate evidence of quality between and among multiple transmedia materials, encouraging critical thinking. Ultimately, this critical thinking process can culminate with the creation of digital read-aloud materials to share with other participants, expressing creativity and agency.

Conclusion

If we can encourage participants to view technology use and quality literature as hand-in-hand companions, that is a positive.

Combining the knowledge supporting traditional read-aloud with the digital read-aloud experience can heighten the engagement of our digital natives. Does this engagement equal learning? It has potential. Deliberate material selections, which require text quality with supportive technologies, can help.

- Quality narration and appropriate dictionary functions (text-embedded definition assistance) are both positive for techno story time.
- Content-connected animations can add to student comprehension of the story and add to positive reader experience.
- Students may not feel the need to turn paper pages or engage in reading in the same way as their parents (Roslund 2012).

We are face-to-face with an evolving generation that views content as the end goal and traditional books as one avenue of reaching that goal. This evolution in thinking can be supported and expanded by the use of digital read-aloud. The expansion of digital read-aloud from passive to active through augmented reality, dynamic dialogue, story author, and code author format could lead to our students being content creators, not just consumers.

Reading aloud can be a shared positive experience that cuts across subject, age, gender, orientation, and demographic differences to create equal-opportunity knowledge growth. Come as you are and where you are to learn together. Why wouldn't we want a communicative experience of this potential magnitude to include our society's greatest contemporary influencer, technology?

Glossary

Acceptable use policy (AUP)
A document stipulating constraints and practices that a user must agree to for access to a network or the Internet.

Audience
The group to which you will be facilitating the digital read-aloud.

Authentic topic
Topic that is research based, real world.

Bookmarking
Tagging pages so that you can return to them at will.

Brains-on
Means that the audience of participants is engaged and ready for the next step.

Critical thinking
The objective analysis and evaluation of an issue in order to form a judgment.

Cross-curricular
Containing the content from more than one discipline.

Digital native
A participant or facilitator who has no recollection of a world without digital technology.

Digital read-aloud
A traditional read-aloud that has been powered up with digital aspects.

Digital world
Time since the advent of technology.

Disabling factor
A functionality that distracts the reader from traveling through the text in an orderly manner.

eBook
A book that can be accessed electronically and can have few or many functionalities.

Enabling factor
A functionality that engages and encourages the reader for traveling through the text.

English-language learners (ELLs)
Participants to whom English is not their first language.

Extension activities
Methods of drawing attention to skill acquisition for digital read-aloud purposes.

Facilitator
The advanced reader who leads the digital read-aloud experience.

Growth mind-set
The state of understanding that there is always room for improvement.

Hands-on
An activity that requires the use of physical manipulation to complete the task.

Heterogeneous
Different configuration of something.

Homogeneous
Same configuration of something.

Hyperlinking
Creating a shortcut to a website that is easily accessible in a document or on a website.

Information
Any knowledge in any format.

Interdisciplinary
The state of containing content from more than one content area.

Interior life
The internal dialogue we all share.

Large group
Five or more participants.

Lizard parenting
Creating something and then walking away to let it fend for itself.

Media multitasking
Using more than one screen device at a time.

Modeling
Displaying a behavior you hope to instill in others.

Multimethod
Employing more than one strategy at a time.

Multimodal
Having more than one mode of activity.

Multiscreen delivery system
Any vehicle for transmedia.

Participant
An individual engaging in the digital read-aloud.

Participant agency
The confluence of motivation, engagement, and voice.

Passive engagement
Watching without any action required.

Personalized learning
An individualized educational experience designed specifically for the individual.

Point-of-need
The moment and location in time when you require assistance.

Positive reinforcement
Noticing the desired behavior and meeting that with praise while ignoring less desirable behavior.

Precorrection
The act of setting the stage for the events to come.

Predigital
Individuals who remember life before computers.

Project-based
Learning that engages students with tasks that lead to learning and problem solving.

Proximity support
Being next to a participant to lend assistance and attention.

Quick response codes (QR codes)
Shortcuts to websites designed to be scanned like a bar code.

Read-aloud
The act of sharing the written word vocally.

Rigor
The difficulty of a thing.

Screen time
Moments spent in front of technology.

Small group
A grouping between two and five.

Social crowd response support
Noting the opinions of others and taking that information as part of a personal truth.

Storytelling
Sharing of knowledge.

Techno-vocabulary
An agreed upon set of terms to allow ease of technology use by group with symbiotic goals.

Transmedia materials
Storytelling across multiple formats.

Universal design for learning (UDL)
The creation of environments that support the comfort and access of all individuals.

Works Cited

Adam, Anna, and Mowers, Helen. 2013. "Should Coding Be the 'New Foreign Language' Requirement?" *Edutopia*. Oct. 30, 2013. <www.edutopia.org/blog/coding-new-foreignlanguage-requirement-helen-mowers> (accessed Sept. 30, 2015).

Adams, M. J. 1990. *Beginning to Read*. Cambridge, MA: MIT Press.

American Association of School Librarians. 2018. "AASL Standards Framework for Learners." <https://standards.aasl.org/framework>

Anderson, Richard C., et al. 1985. "Becoming a Nation of Readers: The Report of the Commission on Reading." <www.eric.ed.gov/PDFS/ED253865.pdf> (accessed Sept. 30, 2015).

Atwell, Nancie. 2007. *The Reading Zone: How to Help Kids Become Skilled, Passionate, Habitual, Critical Readers*. New York: Scholastic.

Big Fish Presentations. 2012. "A Very Brief History of Storytelling." *Big Fish Blog*. Feb. 28, 2012. <http://bigfishpresentations.com/2012/02/28/a-very-brief-history-of-storytelling>

Bishop, Kay, and Cahall, Jenny. 2012. *Positive Classroom Management Skills for School Librarians*. Santa Barbara, CA: Libraries Unlimited.

Campbell, Cen, and Hansen, Genesis. 2014. "Early Literacy Programming in a Digital Age." July 24, 2014. <https://vimeo.com/84698709>

Chisholm, Kate. 2017. "The Lost Pleasure of Reading Aloud." *The Spectator*. Aug. 26, 2017. <https://www.spectator.co.uk/2017/08/the-lost-pleasure-of-reading-aloud>

Data USA: Education, Training and Library Occupations. 2016. <https://datausa.io/profile/soc/250000>

Davis, Julie. 2015. "Classroom Management Tips for the Technology Rich Classroom." *Edutopia*. Feb. 19, 2015. <https://www.edutopia.org/discussion/classroom-management-tips-technology-rich-classroom>

Day, Elizabeth. 2013. "Storytelling: How Reading Aloud Is Back in Fashion." *The Guardian*. Jan. 5, 2013. <https://www.theguardian.com/books/2013/jan/06/storytelling-back-in-fashion>

Delistraty, Cody. 2014. "The Psychological Comforts of Storytelling." *The Atlantic*. <https://www.theatlantic.com/health/archive/2014/11/the-psychological-comforts-of-storytelling/381964>

Duursma, E., Augustyn, B., & Zuckerman, B. 2008. "Reading Aloud to Children: The Evidence." *Arche dis Child* 93.7, 554–557.

Friedman, Barbara. 1997. "The Read-Aloud Event: Three Case Studies: Transaction and Interaction in Three Intermediate Grade Classrooms." PhD diss., University of New Mexico.

Goldfield, B. A., and Snow, C. E. 1984. "Reading Books with Children: The Mechanics of Potential Influence on Children's Reading Achievement." In J. Flood (Ed.), *Promoting Reading Comprehension* (pp. 204–215). Newark, DE: International Reading Association.

Ha, Thu-Huong. 2017. "The Beginning of Silent Reading Changed Westerners' Interior Life." *Quartzy*. Nov. 19, 2017.

Harb, Jennifer K. 2007. "A Lesson Learned: Integrating Literature into the Content Areas." Senior honors thesis. <152.http://commons.emich.edu/honors/152>

Henry J. Kaiser Family Foundation (HKFF). 2010. "Daily Media Use of Children and Teens Up Dramatically from Five Years Ago." Henry J. Kaiser Family Foundation Newsroom. Jan. 20, 2010. <https://www.kff.org/disparities-policy/press-release/daily-media-use-among-children-and-teens-up-dramatically-from-five-years-ago>

Hoffman, James V., Roser, Nancy L., and Battle, Jennifer. 1993. "Reading Aloud in Classrooms: From the Modal toward a 'Model.'" *The Reading Teacher* 46.6 (March), 496–503.

Kagan, Oleg. 2018. "There's Something Wrong with the Library's Image: A Pictorial Guide. It's Not All Books and Shelves at the Library!" *Medium EveryLibrary*. Aug.

Keller, Cynthia. 2012. "Reading Aloud—Why Take the Time." *School Library Monthly* 28.7, 40–41.

Kluger, Jeffrey. 2017. "How Telling Stories Makes Us Human." *Time*. <http://time.com/5043166/storytelling-evolution>

Korbey, Holly. 2018. "Digital Text Is Changing How Kids Read—Just Not in the Way That You Think." KQED Mind Shift. Aug. 21, 2018. <https://www.kqed.org/mindshift/49092/digital-text-is-changing-how-kids-read-just-not-in-the-way-that-you-think>

Krashen, Stephen. 2004. *The Power of Reading: Insights from the Research*, 2nd ed. Westport, CT: Libraries Unlimited.

Marcinek, Andrew. 2014. "Classroom Management in the Tech-Equipped Classroom." *Edutopia*. Sept. 10, 2014. <https://www.edutopia.org/blog/classroom-management-tech-equipped-classroom-andrew-marcinek>

Mendoza, Melissa. 2015. "The Evolution of Storytelling." *Reporter*. May 1, 2015. <https://reporter.rit.edu/tech/evolution-storytelling>

National Center for Educational Statistics (NCES). n.d. *Schools and Staffing Survey (SASS) 2012*. Table 2. Average and median age of public school teachers and percentage distribution of teachers, by age category, sex, and state. <https://nces.ed.gov/surveys/sass/tables/sass1112_2013314_t1s_002 .asp> (accessed June 7, 2018).

Northwest Regional Educational Laboratory (NWREL). n.d. *Literacy Central; Reading Is Fundamental*. <https://www.rif.org/sites/default/files/Support_Materi als/GuidelinesforChoosingRead-AloudBooksforinfantstoddlerspreK.pdf> (accessed Aug. 8, 2018).

Paganelli, A. 2016. "Storytime in a Digital World: Making a Case for Thinking Outside the Book." *Knowledge Quest: Journal of the American Association of School Librarians* 44.3 (Jan./Feb.), 8–17.

Robinson, D. E. 2017. "Universal Design for Learning and School Libraries." *Knowledge Quest* 46.1, 56–61. <http://login.libsrv.wku.edu:2048/login ?url=http://search.ebscohost.com/login.aspx?direct=true&db=a9h&AN =124886372&site=ehost-live>

Rosenthal, Lindsay, and Boser, Ulrich. 2012. "To Improve Schools, We Should Listen to Students." *U.S. News and World Report*. July 10, 2012. <www.us news.com/opinion/articles/2012/07/10/to-improve-schools-we-should -listen-to-students> (accessed Dec. 10, 2016).

Roslund, Samantha. 2012. "Sharpening the Digital Nose: Evaluating eStorybooks." *School Library Monthly* 28.7, 8–10.

Ross, Catherine Sheldrick, McKechnie, Lynne, and Rothbauer, Paulette M. 2006. *Reading Matters: What the Research Reveals about Reading, Libraries, and Community*. Westport, CT: Libraries Unlimited.

Saenger, Paul. 1997. *Space between Words: The Origins of Silent Reading*. Stanford, CA: Stanford University Press.

Starr, Linda. 2013. "Managing Technology Tips from the Experts." *Education World Connecting Educators to What Works*. Jan. 29, 2013. <https://www.education world.com/a_tech/tech/tech116.shtml>

Thorne, James. 2012. "Imag-N-O-Tron: The Augmented Reality Makeover of an Academy Award-Winning Short." *Cool Hunting*. Aug. 3, 2012.

Toppo, Greg. 2015. "How to Build a Better Digital Book." *Atlantic*. July 15, 2015. <www.theatlantic.com/education/archive/2015/07/how-to-build-a-better -digital-book/398567> (accessed Sept. 25, 2015).

Toshalis, Eric, and Nakkula, Michael J. 2012. *Motivation, Engagement, and Student Voice*. Washington, DC: Jobs for the Future and Nellie Mae Education Foundation. <www.nmefoundation.org/resources/youth-develop ment/motivation,-engagement,-and-student-voice> (accessed Dec. 6, 2016).

Tran, Allison. 2014. "A First-Time Digital Storytime Experience." *Little eLit*. April 7, 2014. <http://littleelit.com/2014/04/07/a-first-time-digital-storytime-exper ience-by-allison-tran> (accessed Sept. 25, 2015).

Trelease, Jim. 2013. *The Read-Aloud Handbook*, 7th ed. New York: Penguin.

Vogt, MaryEllen. 1997. "Cross-Curricular Thematic Instruction." <https://www .eduplace.com/rdg/res/vogt> (accessed Aug. 1, 2018).

Further Reading

Biancorosa, Gina, and Griffiths, Gina. 2012. "Technology Tools to Support Reading in the Digital Age." *www.futureofchildren.org* 22.2.

Chartier, Roger. 2017. "6. The Long History of Reading Aloud." *How to Read*. Dec. 6, 2017. <https://www.howtoreadpodcast.com/roger-chartier-history-reading-aloud>

Greenberg, Karin. 2018. "Lesson Plan Ideas for Teaching Information Literacy." *Knowledge Quest Blog*. Sept. 25, 2018. <https://knowledgequest.aasl.org/lesson-plan-ideas-for-teaching-information-literacy>

History.com Editors. 2018. "Welles Scares Nation." HISTORY A&E Television Networks. Aug. 21, 2018. <https://www.history.com/this-day-in-history/welles-scares-nation>

International Society for Technology in Education. 2019. "ISTE Standards." <http://www.iste.org/standards>

Johnson, Spencer, and Ewbank, Ann. 2018. "Heuristics: An Approach to Evaluating News Obtained through Social Media." *Knowledge Quest* 47.1 (Sept./Oct.).

Kelly, Melissa. 2018. "Cross-Curricular Connections in Instruction." June 24, 2018. <https://www.thoughtco.com/cross-curricular-connections-7791>

Lenski, S. D. 2001. "Brain Surfing: A Strategy for Making Cross-Curricular Connections." *Reading Horizons* 42.1. <https://scholarworks.wmich.edu/reading_horizons/vol42/iss1/9>

Lewis, Jan. 2000. "Read Aloud Rubric." <https://community.plu.edu/~lewisjp/408readaloudrubric.htm>

Miller, E. Ce. 2015. "The Open eBooks App Will Allow Children from Low-Income Homes to Access Thousands of Books for Free." *Bustle*. July 20, 2015. <www.bustle.com/articles/98364-the-open-ebooks-app-will-allow-children-from-low-income-homes-to-access-thousands-of-books-for> (accessed Sept. 30, 2015).

National Assessment of Educational Progress (NAEP). n.d. *The Nation's Report Card*. Reading Age 17 Results. <https://www.nationsreportcard.gov/ltt_2012/age17r.aspx> (accessed June 4, 2018).

Shapiro, Jordan. 2018. "The Case for Playing Fortnite with Your Kids Videogames Do Not Represent Our Children's Fall from Grace. It's Time to Get in on the Fun." *Medium EveryLibrary*. Sept.

Wineburg, Sam, et al. 2016. "Evaluating Information: The Cornerstone of Civic Online Reasoning." Stanford Digital Repository. <http://purl.stanford.edu/fv751yt5934>

Index

Academic performance, 3, 49
Acceptable use policy (AUP), 43–45
Advanced reader, 4, 9, 12–13, 21, 58
Agency, 23–24, 47, 51, 52, 59, 77, 89
American Association of School Libraries Learner Standards (AASL), 62
Audience, 8, 18–22, 27, 28, 34, 38, 41, 53
Augmented reality, 27–28, 29, 39, 60, 61, 63
Authentic topic, 22, 25, 35, 36, 38–39, 75, 131
Author, 3, 34, 35, 56

Bookmarking, 43
Brains-on learning, 37, 112

Code author, 24, 27, 28, 29–30, 39, 60
Critical thinking, 23, 37, 107, 133
Cross-curricular learning, 21–23, 24–28, 31, 32, 34, 37–39, 49, 51, 59, 64, 91, 95, 105, 117, 119, 133
   infusion curriculum integration, 39
   infusion integration, 39
   multidisciplinary integration, 39
   parallel integration, 39
   transdisciplinary curriculum integration, 39

Digital native, 11, 17, 59, 135
Digital resource, 27
Digital tradition, 7
Digital world, 13, 17, 73
Dynamic dialogue, 27–29, 39, 60, 63, 65

eBook, 7, 11–12, 14, 28, 31, 32, 38, 53
Elementary school participants, 46
   history/social studies, 110–112
   language arts, 68–70
   math, 82–84
   science, 96–98
   visual performing arts, 124–126
Engagement, 4, 8, 13, 16–18, 22–24, 27–28, 30–38, 42, 43, 45, 47, 49, 51, 53, 56, 59, 64
English-language learners (ELLs), 20, 48
Extension activities, 57–58, 121

Facilitator, 49–52
   coach, 49–50
   principal investigator, 49–50
   project manager, 49–50
   research guide, 49–50
   role, 29–30, 49, 62
Fourth-grade slump, 13, 15

Functions, 28–33, 43–45, 58–59
   considerate, 32–33
   dictionary, 28, 32–34, 59
   disabling factor, 43–45
   enabling factor, 43–45
   inconsiderate, 32–33
   optional quiz, 33

Genre, 3, 6, 31, 34, 35, 36, 38
Growth mind-set, 41, 49

Hands-on learning, 37, 45, 65, 66, 67, 70, 71, 82, 83, 84, 93, 107, 121, 123
Heterogeneous audience, 19
High school participants, 47
   history/social sciences, 114–116
   language arts, 72–75
   math, 86–88
   science, 100–102
   visual performing arts, 128–130
History/social studies, 107–119
   elementary school, 110–112
   high school, 114–116
   lifelong learner, 116–119
   middle school, 112–114
   pre-K, 108–110
Homogeneous audience, 19
Hyperlinking, 43

Illustrator, 3
Information, 4, 6, 7, 8, 11, 13, 14, 17, 19, 20–28, 32–33, 38–39, 48–51, 55, 58, 61–63, 107, 117, 133
Infusion curriculum integration, 39
Infusion integration, 39
Interior life, 6, 7, 13
International Society of Technology in Education (ISTE), 62

Language arts, 65–78
   elementary school, 68–70
   high school, 72–75
   lifelong learner, 75–78
   middle school, 70–72
   pre-K, 65–68
Lifelong learner participants, 47
   history/social sciences, 116–119
   language arts, 75–78
   math, 88–91
   science, 102–105
   visual performing arts, 130–133
Lizard parenting, 58

Math, 79–91
   elementary school, 82–84
   high school, 86–88
   lifelong learner, 88–91
   middle school, 84–86
   pre-K, 80–82
Media multitasking, 16
Media tradition, 6
Middle school participants, 46–47
   history/social sciences, 112–114
   language arts, 70–72
   math, 84–86
   science, 98–100
   visual performing arts, 126–128
Modeling, 12, 15, 20, 29, 50, 54, 113
Motivation, 3, 4, 23–24, 49
Multidisciplinary integration, 39
Multimethod learning, 20, 23
Multimodal resources, 17, 37, 38
Multiscreen delivery system, 32, 42

Oral tradition, 4

Parallel integration, 39
Participant, 4, 7–9, 12–13, 15–25, 27–39, 41–53, 53–59
   agency, 23–24, 51, 52, 77, 90, 104, 118
   analysis, 19–23
   analysis of disposition, 19–20, 23
   analysis of knowledge, 19–23
   diversity, 43, 59

experience, 8–25, 43–59
management, 41–57
population demographics, 18–23, 27, 30, 39, 59
students, 8, 11, 13–14, 17–18, 20, 30, 35, 36, 37, 46–49, 58–60, 64, 68, 70, 77, 84–85, 90, 104, 117–118, 135
Passive engagement, 33
Personalized learning, 21, 23, 29, 30, 36, 49, 65, 79, 87, 90, 93, 101, 108, 121
Point of need, 7, 13, 14, 21, 23
Positive reinforcement, 45
Precorrection, 44, 45, 50, 100, 123
Predigital age adults, 4, 9, 17, 20, 132
Pre-K participants, 45–46
history/social sciences, 108–110
language arts, 65–68
math, 80–81
science, 94–96
visual performing arts, 121–123
Project-based tools, 31
Proximity support, 42

Quick response codes (QR codes), 43

Read-aloud
delivery, 20, 21, 22, 31–36, 42–59
digital, 15–59
diversity, 15–18
evaluation, 53–59
large group, 20–23, 36, 65
management, 41–57
methods, 22, 27, 44–54
one-on-one, 20–21, 36
panacea, 15, 59
planning, 12, 15–25, 27–49
preparation, 8, 15–17, 18–35, 53
quality, 7–17, 25, 32–35, 51–58
reflection, 53–59
schedule, 38–39
small group, 9, 20–21, 23, 28, 29, 30, 36, 51

Reading skills, 3, 13, 51
book mechanics, 3
grammar, 3
letter recognition, 3
story structure, 3
syntax, 3
Rigor, 23

Science, 93–105
elementary school, 96–98
high school, 100–102
lifelong learner, 102–105
middle school, 98–100
pre-K, 94–96
Screen time, 15, 17, 27, 31, 54, 58, 108
Social studies/history, 107–119
elementary school, 110–112
high school, 114–116
lifelong learner, 116–119
middle school, 112–114
pre-K, 108–110
Story author, 24, 27–31, 39
Story elements, 3
Storytelling, 4–7, 13, 28, 74, 75–76, 89, 90, 105, 118, 119, 131, 132
Symbolic tradition, 4–5

Technology
appropriate use, 9, 12–13, 54, 58
availability, 29–30, 38
delivery method, 22, 36, 54, 62
engagement, 3–4, 8, 13, 6–18, 22–27, 28–32
importance, 3–4, 12–13
issues, 3, 7–12
management, 41–45
use, 9–12, 15–17, 44, 59
Techno-vocabulary, 45
Traditional book, 8, 10–12, 38, 58, 60

Transdisciplinary curriculum
    integration, 39
Transmedia, 8, 11–25, 27–59
    choosing, 33–35, 55
    implementation, 41–53
    introduction, 43–45
    selection, 31–35

Universal design for learning (UDL),
    48–49

Visual performing arts, 121–133
    elementary school, 124–126
    high school, 128–130
    lifelong learner, 130–133
    middle school, 126–128
    pre-K, 121–124
Vocabulary, 3, 15, 45, 59
Voice, 8, 21, 23–24, 31, 46, 51, 62

Written tradition, 5

About the Author

Andrea Paganelli is an associate professor at Western Kentucky University. She served as a guest editor for the "Power to the Pupil: Student Agency in the School Library," March/April 2017 issue of *Knowledge Quest*, and wrote the January/February 2016 article "Storytime in a Digital World: Making a Case for Thinking Outside of the Book" for *Knowledge Quest*. Her coauthored publications include "The Makerspace Experience and Teacher Professional Development," "School Library eBook Providers and Spanish Language Equity: An Analysis of eBook Collections Available to School Libraries," and "The Online Embedded Personal Librarian Approach to Providing Reference Services via a Course Management System."